Exploring Shamanism

Using Ancient Rites
to Discover the
Unlimited Healing
Powers of Cosmos
and Consciousness

by

Hillary S. Webb

New Page Books
A Division of Career Press Inc.
Franklin Lakes, NJ

Copyright © 2003 by Hillary S. Webb

EXPLORING SHAMANISM
EDITED BY JODI BRANDON
TYPESET BY KRISTEN PARKES
Cover design by The Visual Group
Cover art: Woman with Bird, Susan Cohen Thompson
(www.thompsonartstudio.com)
Printed in the U.S.A. by Book-mart Press

To order this title, please call toll-free 1-800-CAREER-1 (NJ and Canada: 201-848-0310) to order using VISA or MasterCard, or for further information on books from Career Press.

The Career Press, Inc., 3 Tice Road, PO Box 687,
Franklin Lakes, NJ 07417
www.careerpress.com
www.newpagebooks.com

Library of Congress Cataloging-in-Publication Data

Webb, Hillary S., 1971-

Exploring Shamanism : using ancient rites to discover the unlimited healing powers of cosmos and consciousness / by Hillary S. Webb.

p. cm.

Includes index.

ISBN 1-56414-663-4 (pbk.)

1. Shamanism. I. Title.

BL2370.S5W43 2003

291.1'44--dc21

2003051275

To

Maddi Wallach.

teacher, friend, humble seeker

and

to

Carl Hyatt,

who wants to know things.

Acknowledgments

First and foremost, thanks must go to my agent, Stephany Evans, for bringing this project to my attention and for convincing me that I might just have something to say on the subject. Thanks to New Page Books for agreeing with her.

Thanks and appreciation go to those who read the manuscript in its various stages. These people acted as another set of eyes to see past the places where my own perspective stopped short: Dennis Perrin, Carl Hyatt, Evelyn Rysdyk, Maddi Wallach, Cheryl Krisko, Alex Stark, and, of course, my editor, Jodi Brandon. Thank you all.

Many thanks to Susan Cohen Thompson for allowing me to use her beautiful piece, "Woman with Bird," on the cover of this book. As good art so often does, her painting sums up in an instant what it took me close to 60 thousand words to write.

Certain individuals, both directly and simply by nature of their existence, have been indispensable to this project and to my life. These include: Pam Broido, Leslie Adams, Carl Hyatt, Maddi Wallach, Dennis and Aimee Perrin, Beth Welwood, Bonnie Bufkin, Jennifer Macaluso, and Steve Pellicci. Of extra special mention in this category, thanks and love go to my mother and sister, who have been my greatest sources of love, support, and confidence throughout my life. Although they did not know it, a big part of the reason I took on this project was that it provided me a way of explaining just what their crazy daughter and sister had been up to for the last several years. Thank you both for being my involuntary muses.

Perhaps most importantly, I would like to extend my most heartfelt appreciation to my teachers in this work, who have guided me through the practice, including all the shamans and shamanic practitioners from various parts of the world who took the time to share their knowledge with me during our conversations over the past several years. I would also like to acknowledge my teachers and allies in the spirit realms, those who have guided me through this project and this life so exquisitely, and who have revealed to me, little by little and all at once, the magic and beauty that exist within the many worlds of consciousness.

And, finally, thanks go to my father for teaching me the magic of words.

Table of Contents

Foreword

In spite of our many extraordinary advances and discoveries, western culture has largely forgotten the greatest wisdom of our ancestors: that all of Nature is alive, essential, and interdependent. The widespread degradation of the Earth's environment and many of today's illnesses stem from human beings falling out of harmony with the rest of Creation. In our excitement to move ahead—preoccupied with our own species' desires above all others—we have forgotten our place in the Whole. Like runaway toys, we have stretched beyond the limits of our cord and pulled our own plug. In order to come back to life—to come back into a oneness with power—we need to find a way to reconnect ourselves.

Shamanic cultures arose during the time when our species engaged in hunting and gathering as a means for survival. During that time, we lived lightly and with respect to the other beings with whom we shared the land, taking only what we needed to survive. Humans lived in small, temporary sleeping/cooking camps and set out each morning, on foot, to accumulate that which was necessary for the day. Upon completing these tasks, our ancestors would once again return to the encampment to share the bounty. Every member was essential, and the actions of each person contributed to the ultimate survival and welfare of the whole.

There was often one member of the group whose duties included gathering those necessities that were not readily accessible using ordinary means. If, for instance, one of the band was lost or ill, this was an urgent situation requiring immediate attention. If the means to solve the problem couldn't be found by using ordinary methods, the shaman would be called into service. The role of the shaman was to access that which was outside of the usual realm of human perception. To embark on this highly specialized work of survival, the shaman would, in some way, alter consciousness to engage in a form of spirit travel called a shamanic journey. Having accessed the required information, the shaman would then return to implement what she or he had discovered—reflecting the familiar hunter/gatherer rhythm. This visionary technique was so successful that it spread wherever the people wandered across the globe.

Today, we are at another juncture where the survival of our species is in question. Once again, sheer necessity is pressuring us to find a way to reach beyond our perceptual limitations. Perhaps the most ancient of our spiritual traditions can provide us with the methods to escape the snare of our own destruction and find a way to re-create the fertile garden of our origins.

It isn't surprising that the path of the shaman has been referred to as a Way of the Heart. Cutting-edge science has proven that it is our heart that broadcasts the energy of our feelings out into the world, and these energies actually affect the physical state of those around us. These broadcast energies either disrupt or support the continuity of life. In laboratory tests, scientists have shown that our emotions actually change the configuration of DNA, both in our own bodies and in those of the beings that surround us. The configuration of the DNA reflects the degree of cellular functionality available to the organism. In the presence of love, compassion, or gratitude, our DNA and that found in our fellow beings returns to full function and balance. Clearly these emotions are the most harmonious with the vibrations of Creation. Research has proven the truth shamans have always known: that our heart is our center and, through acting with love, compassion, and gratitude, we contact the Divine.

Exploring Shamanism presents the reader with an opportunity to enter back into a heartfelt relationship with the spirits with whom we share this wonderful world. Offering to guide the reader through the shamanic realms, Hillary S. Webb helps you to awaken the knowledge that compassionate, loving, and powerful spirits are everywhere. As a reader, you have the opportunity to remember that no one is ever alone or separate and that every part of creation has its own power. You can begin to feel the pulsing of every tree, stone, river, and living being, recalling the sheer awesomeness and remarkable sanctity of Life. As awareness blossoms, through study, practicing the exercises in this book, and prayer, something else may begin to grow inside your heart, as well. Deep memories of your own sacredness may begin to surface.

Imagine how the world will be when every one of us recognizes that every being—including ourselves—is a precious part of creation! As each person recalls the heart-centered ways of the shaman and utilizes the power of the shamanic journey, we, as a species, will reclaim our relationship with the spirits, regain humility, and reveal the path to healing ourselves, our communities, and the planet as a whole.

Evelyn C. Rysdyk
Author, *Modern Shamanic Living*

Introduction

L ife is full of moments of quiet revelation, some so small that they are barely noticeable, others so profound that you emerge with all preconceived notions of reality and yourself changed forevermore. On these occasions, one is faced with a choice: disregard the experience out of fear or cynicism, or allow its momentum to open you up to even greater possibilities for the world and yourself. In the fall of 1999, revelation came to me in the form of an oyster shell sticking up out of the mud in a riverbed in Asbury, New Jersey. It was a discovery that not only reshaped the path that my career has taken, but forever altered the way I look at the world and my place in it.

Throughout my life, I have been drawn to study philosophies and religions of all kinds. As a child growing up in Salem, Massachusetts, I was especially compelled by the practices of people who directed their spiritual yearning toward the earth instead of outwards toward some unseen and elusive God.

For these people, the creative force of the universe was not off somewhere in the clouds, but a tangible part of the physical world, accessible to everyone at any time. What's more, in their world, "magic" was not just some flight-of-fancy, limited to fairy tales and superstition, but the result of an actual energy existing around us that could be harnessed and used. My young mind was intrigued and inspired by this, and a longing was born inside me. I became obsessed with the idea that there might be more to the world around me than most people would acknowledge. I was fortunate to live where I did. As the site of the infamous Salem Witch Trials and, in more recent years, a kind of mecca for those involved in alternative spiritualities, enough information was made available to keep that fire burning within me well stoked. Whenever I could, I would walk into town to scour the witch's markets, bookstores, and library for information on astral projection, ESP, reincarnation—any subject that had to do with the mystical or metaphysical.

At the time, my goal was to unlock the secrets of the universe. Only now, as an adult, do I see that what I was really trying to do was unlock the mystery of me and, with it, my place within the universe at large.

My passion for mystical exploration led me throughout my life, ebbing somewhat in my teenage years, as boys suddenly became the most mysterious things in the universe, then resurfacing with a fury in adulthood. After graduating from journalism school in New York and landing a job as a staff writer at an alternative weekly magazine in New Mexico, I used my position to finagle interviews and attend seminars on metaphysical subjects by persuading my editor to let me write articles on them. At that same time, I found a group of people who had similar interests, with whom I began sharing ideas and experiences. Once a month, we would gather at the foothills of the Sandia Mountains in Albuquerque and do rituals that we created for ourselves. There, under the full moon, with the light of the fire casting long pagan shadows across the desert sand, we propelled ourselves out of the ordinary world and into the realm of the numinous.

In my mid-20s, after moving back to New England, I found another group of spiritually minded people to connect to. One of them was studying shamanism, a practice I had heard of but knew very little about. On his recommendation, I attended a seminar that was being given on the subject. I was immediately captivated by the teachings.

Shamanism is an immensely ancient practice that is believed to be no less that 31,000 years old, dating back well into Paleolithic times.[1] Shamanism is, in fact, considered by many religious historians to be the "proto-religion"—the world's first method of engaging with the sacred, which broke up into various distinctive practices and eventually evolved and shifted into what are today the world's major religions. Despite this evolution, as well as the attempted desecration of it by invading cultures, the soul of the shamanic worldview survived intact. Today, many indigenous cultures throughout the world still use shamanism as their primary spiritual practice. What's more, anthropologists have noted amazing consistencies in the philosophy and practices of these shamanic cultures, despite its appearance in such geographically diverse places as Europe, Africa, Asia, Australia, and the Americas.

According to the beliefs of this ancient spiritual tradition, there are worlds that exist beyond physical reality that are hidden to everyday, ordinary consciousness. Within these realms live spiritual entities, both benevolent and destructive, that have the ability to help or hinder the fates of those living in the physical world. Even the world of "ordinary" reality is, according to these belief systems, a hidden world to most people. Shamanism is a spirituality of animism, the belief that all forms of matter, from humans to animals to plants to rivers to the stars in the sky and everything in between, have their own innate consciousness and intelligence.

In shamanic philosophy, "All is One," and each of these entities is seen as an essential piece of the puzzle that is the cosmos, indispensable strands in the web of life that binds the world together and emanates from one great Creator Spirit.

Our ancient ancestors living in close connection to the natural world realized that communications and interactions with the forces of the unseen world were essential for the survival and prosperity of the community. Because of this, they were required to seek out those individuals who possessed the ability to engage and interact with the forces of nature and the gods and demons that were believed to control their fates. Their very survival in the physical world depended on it. These unique individuals, today called shamans, had the ability (either through training or through a natural predisposition) to enter into altered states of consciousness in which they were said to release the soul (or, in some cases, a part of the soul) from their body, allowing them to enter into the invisible realms at will. There, the shaman would make contact with personal helping spirits in order to access any manner of extrasensory information or power that was needed. In his authoritative study, *Shamanism: Archaic Techniques of Ecstasy*, historian Mircea Eliade called the shamans "technicians of ecstasy" and "masters of the spirits." With this otherwise inaccessible knowledge and power, the shaman was able to glean information about proper hunting methods, gain control over the forces of weather, divine the future or the past, heal the sick, interpret dreams—anything that was deemed necessary for sustaining the health and survival of the community.

Despite the fact that these practices were once (and still are by many people) considered "superstition" and the shamans that performed them "ministers of the devil," today people from non-indigenous, westernized cultures have turned to these teachings as a viable spiritual and healing path. In fact, many leading health professionals who typically use more "standard," allopathic treatment have, in recent years, begun incorporating the healing practices and modalities of shamanic cultures into their work.

In the workshop I attended, the instructor showed us a technique called "Shamanic Journeying," a means of accessing these altered states of consciousness similar to the methods used by indigenous shamans by going into a deep meditative state. In order to journey in this way, one must make a transition from the ego-centered left-brain process that controls logical thinking (the dominant function in most western cultures) to the expansive right brain, believed to be responsible for intuition and symbolic thinking, as well as moments of revelation.

Although my first journey didn't result in any kind of spectacular vision that I had hoped for, I was intrigued nonetheless. I was deeply fascinated by the idea that, through various techniques, one could drop the ego mind and propel one's consciousness out of the rut of ordinary consensual reality that it is normally locked into, thereby tapping into a source of knowledge that emanates from the spirit world. The possibility of this kind of direct revelation was breathtaking, and exactly what I had been looking for. Unlike many religious or spiritual practices I had encountered, in shamanism there are no scrolls or scriptures dictating "truth." In this approach to the numinous, faith is—to a certain extent, at least—taken out of the equation. There is no need for faith, for shamanism provides tools and techniques that make it possible for anyone to have empirical proof of its teachings. The "truth" one seeks is found directly, through personal exploration in sacred relationship with the spirits that are always around us waiting to be called upon.

And so I began studying shamanism, taking workshops with different teachers from various traditions. I jumped into it as kind of a smorgasbord, trying a little from each tradition to see what each had to offer. In addition to studying with teachers from the United States, I made a number of trips to South America and Central America to study with medicine people of Peru and Mexico. There I witnessed shamanic healings and participated in some awe-inspiring rituals led by native shamans, but, although I had a number of moving experiences during that time, my grasp of the subject remained mostly on an intellectual and theoretical level. I still felt like an outside observer looking in.

Ironically, despite all my trips to exotic locations, my awakening experience—that which transformed my experience of shamanism from that of intellectual curiosity to a calling of my heart—came to me in the backwoods of New Jersey, U.S.A.

It was late November, and I was attending a weeklong workshop taught by a man who had, as a child, been the apprentice of an Apache elder. This particular workshop was dedicated to learning how to enter into shamanic states of consciousness. For the better part of a week, my fellow students and I lay on our backs in the middle of the woods, learning how to go into these altered states through specialized meditations. One day, before beginning the meditations, the teacher told us to go into the woods and to find a trail that we'd never been down before. We were instructed not to walk down the trail, but to simply take note of it. Back at the workshop site, he then led us into a journey in which we were, in our minds' eye, standing at the head of that same trail. We envisioned ourselves walking down it, taking note of all the things we "saw" there. In my journey, I found myself walking down a tree-lined path that suddenly opened up to...a beach! I felt frustrated with this image because, as my logical, linear mind reasoned, there was no ocean out here in the middle of the woods. The instructor had warned us that some of the images might not make sense at first and to ignore the part of our minds that told us that we were "wrong." I kept going and let myself enjoy the experience. As I walked, I look down and found a large oyster shell at my feet.

The meditation continued for several moments until the facilitator brought us out. He then instructed us to go back to the trail and, this time, physically walk down it. I did so, not feeling too confident that my journey was anything more than the aimless ramblings of my own imagination. As it turned out, the trail, which was like any trail in any woods that one might find, opened up to a stream. At the banks of the stream, half buried in the mud, was the same oyster shell that I had seen in my journey.

A feeling—one a lot like relief—poured through me. In hindsight, I realize that that feeling was similar to that of a child lost in a supermarket that has finally found her mother again. Although the experience of finding the shell didn't exactly prove the existence of God per se, it did give me the proof that I had been looking for since childhood that there was much more to the world, and to ourselves, than our physical experience of it. The fact that I had done it myself proved that we all—not just indigenous people brought up in these traditions from birth—have the ability to step outside of our ordinary consciousness to access a state in which Newtonian laws of science no longer seem to apply. I had glimpsed the power of this practice and, along with that, the possibilities for our unlimited potential within these altered states of consciousness that the shamans, these "technicians of ecstasy," have been masters of for thousands of years. This realization left me high on the possibilities. I wondered: If that kind of "knowing" was possible, how far could I—or anyone else, for that matter—go with these practices?

From that moment on I began intense research into the teachings of shamanism. I continued to study with teachers from various traditions and broadened my studies to include institutes dealing with the exploration of human consciousness. As a way of furthering my understanding, I spent a year and a half interviewing more than two dozen shamans from around the world, both those with native roots as well as those born in the west who have embraced and adopted the teachings into their own philosophy and practice. This in itself was an amazing experience, as it gave me an opportunity to sit down and talk with some of the most insightful shamanic writers, teachers, and visionaries of our time. The conversations (which will be published in the book *Traveling Between the Worlds: Conversations on Contemporary Shamanism* in the summer of 2004), combined with my own personal experiences in this work, became the basis of this book that you have before you. Parts of many of those conversations are included here as a way of bringing together voices from various shamanic traditions.

I have taken the title of this book, *Exploring Shamanism*, quite literally. For me, the journey of writing this book has been exactly that: an exploration. It has been an opportunity to take a scattered collection of ideas and information and synthesize them into a cohesive whole. Putting it together became like sifting through pieces of a three-dimensional jigsaw puzzle, fitting them together, and seeing the amazing shapes that could be formed. Each chapter in the book has been another piece of that puzzle and, through the process of trying to explain it to others, a number of concepts that had eluded me for years became clearer. Knowing how essential personal experience is to the work, each chapter is followed by experiential exercises geared towards releasing old thought patterns and ways of being that may act as a hindrance to getting into a shamanic state of consciousness. Because at this point in my life I do not practice the teachings of any one particular tradition, most of the exercises given are not specifically shamanic in nature (meaning they do not necessarily come out of the teachings of any specific tradition). Certainly, these exercises are in no way meant to take the place of a teacher in this work. Simply completing the exercises outlined here will not make you a shaman. The exercises are instead meant to provide an opportunity to explore your own mental processes and give you a taste of the beauty of this work. As we will see, "knowing thyself" is the first step in helping you shake loose from ordinary patterns of thought that may be preventing you from freely exploring the limitlessness of the universe and of your-self. They can also be helpful in laying the foundation for further practice in shamanism should you choose to follow the path.

As author Tom Cowan wrote in his beautiful book, *Fire in the Head*:

> In order to journey into other realms, we must do more than get out of the body; we must get out of the head. The shaman is a master of escaping the mind-body matrix that characterizes ordinary consciousness and entering the shamanic or non-ordinary state consciousness. In this dreamlike state, the imaginal realm reshapes itself, creating a placeless, timeless field in which the shaman can participate.[2]

And we can all participate in this shift of consciousness, at least to some extent, whether we call ourselves shamans, shamanic practitioners,[3] or simply humble seekers. In fact, I deeply believe that we must. We as a collective culture have reached a place in our evolution where we need a new paradigm, a new vision, in which to relate to the world around us. The old ways of looking at the world—and ourselves as separate from it—are no longer working for us. Today we look out at a world in which we are faced with rising levels of environmental degradation and an epidemic of melancholy among our people. It has been said that you cannot change a situation with the same consciousness that created it. If we are to find new ways of looking at the world and ourselves, we must reclaim that part of ourselves that is free to travel the cosmos and gain new insights and understanding from the divine universe in which we live. It is our birthright, handed down to us from our ancient Paleolithic ancestors. It is contained within our DNA. We just need to learn how to access it. The teachings of shamanism can help us do just that.

It is no accident, I think, that interest in shamanism has grown to the extent that it has over the last several decades. Today, great numbers of westerners are spending hundreds upon thousands of dollars each year on workshops and books dedicated to giving non-indigenous people an experience of this ancient tradition. What was once considered a "low level" religion has today become downright trendy.

I can't help but think this is a good thing. Every book, every seminar and workshop, is a teaching that, if the resonance is there, can be likened to pulling up the window shades in a very dark room. The more light that comes into that room—or the more perspectives that are articulated on any one subject—the clearer the details become. It is for this same reason that in this book I use the metaphors of science, psychology, and mythology in order to explain certain principles of shamanism. Some would argue against this technique, believing that spirituality should not be "explained away" by scientific or psychological paradigms. I agree with this in so much as there are many whose aim it is to discount the spiritual experience by regarding it as simply a series of psychological or physiological dysfunction or disturbances and therefore not "real" or, at least, an experience that is limited solely to the inner, rather than an energy existing outside of us. Although there is undeniably a psychological and physiological process that occurs during the spiritual experience (as we will continue to look at throughout the book), one can also take the perspective that these processes are *reflective* of the spiritual experience, not negating of it. Besides that, we will come to see that what shamans have known for thousands of years, modern science and psychology are now beginning to understand. Or, if not understand, then at least to accept. What appears to be "magic" and "miracles" and beyond the realm of the rational begins to make sense under the paradigm of the new physics that reveals a deeply connected, non-local universe in which old assumptions of cause and effect have been completely shattered. The concept of a holographic universe is also central to this book, a scientific theory that perfectly reflects the age-old Hermetic axiom of "As Above, So Below." According to the holographic model, every piece of the universe contains the intelligence of the whole. Just as our DNA contains a reflection of us as individuals, so too do we as individuals reflect the cosmos. Nineteenth-century occultist Eliphas Levi summed up this concept when he wrote in *Dogma y Ritual de La Alta Magia*, "The soul of man is a magical mirror into the universe."

The goal behind this book is to bring as much light into that darkened room as possible. *Exploring Shamanism* is dedicated to highlighting the major themes and practices inherent in all shamanic traditions, as well as how these same principles are reflected in our modern paradigms of science, psychology, and mythology. The chapters focus on the shaman's philosophy and practices, his or her role within the community, and the way in which those of us in non-shamanic societies can utilize these concepts ourselves. The difficulty in such an undertaking has been trying to show shamanism in both its unity and its diversity—that is, wanting to define these terms as broadly as possible in order to do justice to the myriad forms that shamanism takes throughout the world, but specifically enough that one can gain an understanding into the common themes and philosophies inherent in most, if not all, shamanic traditions.

What I bring to the writing of this book is a deep love for this ancient spirituality in all its myriad forms. My belief is that by embracing reality as it is seen through the lens of the shaman, all of us can experience ourselves as vital strands in the great web of life, as reflections of the greater whole that is the divine cosmos. By holding this truth, we hold the knowledge of lifetimes and awaken ourselves to a world without limits.

Chapter 1

Mapping the Cosmos: Axis Mundi and the Shamanic Worldview

When one is about to make a journey into an unfamiliar land, the first thing one must do is consult a map in order to become familiar with the terrain into which one will travel. The same is true of anyone entering the world of the shaman. In order to fully understand the shaman's roles in any given community, the "magical" skills that he or she possesses, the journeys that he or she undertakes in order to acquire knowledge, and the doctrines that dictate his or her moral codes, one must consider the worldview that shapes the shaman's vision of the cosmos. The cosmology of any spiritual practice reveals its soul and is the basis on which all other beliefs, techniques, powers, and abilities are achieved.

Sacred Architecture: The 3 Worlds, 4 Directions, and the Central Axis of the World

According to the shamanic vision of reality, the cosmos is divided into a series of subtle planes of existence, of which our current reality is just one. As do notes on the harmonic scale, each of these planes contains its own unique vibration and resonance, the total sum of which make up the vast symphony that is the universe. All through the world, the creation stories of many spiritual traditions reflect that matter and life began with God's tones and sounds. People of Southeast Asia call it *Nada Brahma*, the Great Tone from which God made the world.[1] In Egyptian lore, the original god Khepri created first himself and then brought the world into form by calling out his own name.[2] Even our modern science is coming to a similar conclusion. Modern particle physics and quantum mechanics are finding that the ultimate ground of being—all the matter, sounds, and color that make up our physical reality—are nothing more than wave vibrations that have manifested into physical form.

Although these planes of reality are infinite and, therefore, cannot truly be separated into isolated parts, for practical purposes, most shamanic traditions divide the cosmos into three separate but interpenetrating realms, designated as the Lower World, Middle World, and Upper World. Just as choral sections are divided up into alto, mezzo, and soprano, each of these worlds is viewed by some as holding a different vibrational pattern and resonance. Through self-induced states of ecstasy—trances—the shaman's mind becomes a radio to attune to the frequencies of the universe. In these states, a kind of "sympathetic resonance"[3] occurs. The shaman's soul, released from the confines of the physical, ascends or descends into one or more of these worlds by way of the *axis mundi*, the center pillar of the world. As in a dream, the shaman journeys into lands in which every feature is imbued with allegorical significance, lands that often bear a striking resemblance to our own, but in which the laws of nature and time are suspended, where life is recognizable but changed in unusual ways. Animals, people, and places that would be considered mythological or imaginary in an ordinary state of consciousness exist in a very real way in the context of these other worlds. Likewise, in traveling within these realms, the shaman steps out of linear, causal time and into a place where time and space, cause and effect, cease to exist. In this state, it is not unusual for the shaman to encounter the spirits of the dead who exist simultaneously on these other planes. In these worlds, the shaman comes in contact with his or her helping spirits, who provide him or her with the information and power needed for healing, knowledge, and growth in order to evoke change in the physical world.[4]

The exact descriptions of each of the three worlds tend to be culturally specific and change in detail from tradition to tradition, individual to individual, thereby making an exact template of each world impossible. Still, certain archetypal patterns emerge when one shaman's experience is compared to the other, indicating that the specific characteristics of each world go well beyond an individual or particular cultural belief system. The following descriptions of each of the three worlds, although by no means complete or exact, come from a distillation of some of the congruent characteristics throughout a number of traditions and experiences.

The Lower World

Many shamans experience the Lower World as a place of spiritual regeneration. The Lower World is often symbolized by the snake, which sheds its skin over and over, constantly renewing itself to be born again. In the Lower World, writes Mircea Eliade, "rivers flow backward to their sources,"[5] implying that this is the place of beginnings, the place of origins, a dark fertile realm in which the seeds of all life and creativity are nourished and nurtured.

Following the cyclical nature of the world, the place of beginnings naturally corresponds with the place of endings— and beginnings then again. We see this in the life cycle of a flower, which grows from a seed in the dark earth, springs forth into the light, drops its seed, and then disintegrates back into the earth to become a part of it again. This is why, as we will see in Chapter 2, a journey to the Lower World is vital for the shamanic initiate before any level of mastery can be achieved. In the Lower World, the neophyte encounters his or her allies of that realm, such as power animals, who aid in his or her quest for knowledge and empower the shaman to face the internal and external challenges of shedding his or her "skin"— beliefs, paradigms, prejudices—with courage.

In her book, *Riding Wind Horses*, Mongolian shaman Sarangerel gives this description of the Lower World as it is viewed by her people:

> The lower world is basically similar to this world except that the inhabitants have only one soul, rather than the three possessed by human beings.... The ami soul, which causes breathing and warmth in the body, is lacking, so lower-world dwellers are cold and have dark blood. Furthermore, some of the dwellers in the lower world are actually the suns souls of human beings awaiting reincarnation. The sun and moon of the lower world are not as bright as this world; the Samoyed say it is because the sun and moon of the lower world are actually half, rather than full, orbs. The lower world has forests, mountains, and settlements, just like this world, and its inhabitants even have their own shamans. The ruler of the lower world is Erleg Khan, son of Father Heaven. He has authority over the disposition of souls, when and where they will incarnate. Shamans often must appeal to him when recovering souls that have prematurely wandered away to the lower world before the body has died. Outside of these situations, people from the middle world rarely enter the realm of Erleg Khan, except after death.[6]

In his or her journeys, the shaman typically accesses the Lower Worlds through a hole in the ground, often at the roots of a tree. Other descension points include caves, animal holes, and even bodies of water such as lakes or oceans. Among Native American shamans the entrance may be a hot spring or the circular kivas of the Zuni Indians.[7] However, although holes located in various natural settings are typical archetypes for entry into the Lower World, the manner of descent can look like anything that the mind can conceive of. (During one of my own journeys to the Lower World, I found myself descending by way of a department store escalator!)

In its most negative context, the Lower World has been associated in the Christian tradition as Hell, a place of infinite suffering from which all evil and ills of the world stem. Although the Lower World can be a place of difficult challenges and trials, as well as beauty, shamanic philosophy does not consider such adversities to be purely "good" or "evil." In fact, shamanism in general rejects the idea of dualism as opposing forces and instead considers them to be what in the Peruvian tradition is called *yanantin*: complementary opposites. Light and dark, creation and destruction—each are a part of the twofold and complementary character of the universe that can be likened to two sides of a coin: Each exists only in relation with the other, inseparable, interdependent, and in a continual state of interchange. The universe depends on it, for the rhythm of the world is the rhythm of their alterations.

In science, this idea is reflected in the existence of matter and antimatter.[8] As physicist Niels Bohr said in describing what he called the "principal of complementary":

> You can't define the nature of one thing without reference to its complementary opposite. Good and bad, up and down, left and right—all these complementary concepts can be understood only in terms of their relationship to each other. What does up mean without

down, or good without bad? You can't have one without the other: otherwise you can have no frame of
reference to compare concepts to.[9]

All things shape the universe, and in the shamanic vision
of the world even those things that cause discomfort or pain
have their own place in the cosmic order. Although the ideas
of creation and destruction seem to be opposites, within the
natural flow of the universe they never truly conflict—except
in the perception of our own minds and ego limitations—
because there is always a period of change, a turning point in
which one flows into the other. All things, individuals, times,
and spaces are at some stage in the process of being created
and other times destroyed and re-created again.

As Tom Cowan said during one of our talks:

In the ancient Irish myths, the Fomorians—the so-called
"evil" gods of chaos, of destruction, of "unmaking"—
are not evil in the sense that they should be destroyed.
You don't necessarily like what they do, because they're
always destructive and violent, but there's a role for
them. You have to work with them. They are part of
the Shapers. In the Bible, the Genesis story says the
God created us out of nothing. The Celtic way of looking at it is to say that God created us out of himself. In
fact *Cruthaitheair*, the Gaelic Word for "Creator," really means "Shaper." It's the sense that there are powers, or maybe one divine power, that are continually
shaping and reshaping all things of nature and our
world—including us. So even the destructive aspects
of nature, like the Fomorians, come from the same
source. In each of us there is a Fomorian strain that
might be the cause of our anger, our resentments, our
blow-ups, and our self-destructive impulses. Then, because the shaman is concerned with healing power, he
or she will, at some point, discover the power that
exists within this part of us as well. The shaman must

then decide how to transform the so-called "negative" energy so that it can be made to work towards the whole, towards healing, and for doing good work.[10]

Despite a certain amount of acceptance of such things, this is not to suggest that shamanic wisdom condones complacency in our response to what we might consider "evil." Quite the contrary. At the bottom of it all, the function of the shaman is to act as a balancing point between the two parts of creation, between chaos and order, ensuring that one does not outweigh the other. The task of the shaman is to integrate these seemingly opposing forces, to negotiate this cosmic dance and use such "negative" forces as a reservoir of energy to be harnessed, just as in all creation myths chaos was brought to cosmic order under the influence of spirit. Much like in the familiar Serenity Prayer, the shaman, through his or her skills and training—and with assistance from spirit allies—seeks the wisdom to change what can and must be changed to ensure this balance and yet accept those things that, although difficult, exist naturally within the flow of the universe.

Distinguishing between the voice of spirit and that part of us rooted in the ego that may wish to twist and manipulate the world to our own benefit is very often one of the shaman's greatest challenges. As we will see in the next chapter, it is often through a spiritual or physical crisis that forces the neophyte shaman to face his or her darker impulses that the individual finds purity of thought and action, for to know the darkness within and without is the only way to recognize and utilize this energy and transmute it into a power that can be used for the good of all.

The Upper World

The Upper World is considered by some to be a realm of high vibration and bears a close resemblance to the Christian notion of a celestial Heaven as a place of light and love. The

Mongolian-Buryat tradition calls it the "Place of the Seven Suns,"[11] a place of intense brightness, perhaps brought about by its high vibrational pattern. Large birds often act as representatives for the Upper World, such as the eagle for the Native Americans, the vulture in the Tibetan Bon tradition, and the condor to the people of the Andes, as they are considered messengers of the Great Spirit and symbols of transcendence. From their place in the sky, soaring above the earth with an all-encompassing view, they can see with clarity and totality. At times the shaman may ascend to the Upper World on the back of one of these birds or even transform into one him or herself. Other common methods of ascent to the Upper World include a ladder, a rainbow, or up the branches of a tree. The means by which one can make such a journey are, of course, infinite.

The Upper World is often seen as the place of our higher consciousness. It is here that we may have the opportunity to connect with our divine selves, with the Creator, and with all beings of all higher knowledge. In this realm, the shaman will often encounter teachers in human form, sometimes gods or demi-gods, supreme beings, or divine ancestors.

One of the most famous examples of an Upper World journey is that of the Sioux holy man Black Elk. In the book, *Black Elk Speaks*, Black Elk tells of the "Great Vision" that he experienced as a boy during an intense sickness:

> I can see out through the opening [of the teepee], and there two men were coming from the clouds, headfirst like arrows slanting down, and I knew they were the same that I had seen before. Each now carried a long spear, and from the points of these a jagged lightning flashed. They came clear down to the ground this time and stood a little way off and looked at me and said: "Hurry! Come! Your Grandfathers are calling you!"[12]

Black Elk goes on to describe how the two men then left the ground "like arrows slanting upwards from the bow."

Suddenly, he no longer felt ill and instead felt very light. Outside the teepee, a cloud came towards him and lifted him up into the sky into a place "where white clouds were piled like mountains on a wide blue plain, and in them the thunder beings lived and leaped and flashed." His journey continues with the sudden appearance of "the being with four legs," a bay horse with whom he travels even further into the celestial realms.

Black Elk's vision is a wonderful example of an Upper World journey, as it reflects much of the iconography that corresponds to indigenous traditions around the world. Heavenly signs and signals, such as thunder and lightning, are associated with these celestial journeys and, as in Black Elk's case, are very often a sign from spirit that the neophyte has been chosen to be initiated onto the shamanic path. The horse has been seen in some indigenous cultures as a funerary animal, to have the ability to pass from this world into the next with ease, and therefore can play a role in the shaman's entrance into ecstasy. Siberian cultures would often sacrifice a horse so that the shaman's soul could "hitch a ride," so to speak, on the horse's soul during its celestial journey.[13]

Black Elk is brought by the bay horse to meet with the "Six Grandfathers," who, he comes to understand, represent the six "Powers of the World": North, South, East, West, Sky, and Earth. As he passes before them, each of the Six Grandfathers gives Black Elk gifts to aid him in his pursuit of growth and learning and knowledge: a cup of water, bows and arrows, the "white wing of cleansing," a healing herb, the sacred pipe, and a "flowering stick."

During a journey to any of the three worlds, it is common for the shaman to be given gifts of varying natures by his or her spirit allies. These gifts hold personal messages for the individual and, although not "tangible" in the physical sense, hold tremendous power and transformative abilities as symbolic representations. These gifts are to be carried into the physical world not by the hand, but by the heart. In Black Elk's case, the bows and arrows, along with the sacred objects of healing and cleansing, represent the shaman's greatest gift and burden: the power to make live as well as destroy. It is by consulting with his or her spirit allies that the shaman is granted the clarity and vision to see the difference between the two.

The Middle World

The Middle World is the world of the physical, the one that we are attuned to when we are awake. The Maya call it *kai-uleu*—"The Sky-Earth Place." For most of us, this world is made up principally of those things that we see with our eyes, hear with our ears, and taste with our tongues, the odors that we smell via the olfactory nerves, and the sensations we receive though our nerve endings. But although most of our conscious experience of the world is limited and defined by the input from our five senses, the shaman's perceptual state goes beyond those limitations and opens up to take in the images and experiences that his or her special training awakens his or her eyes to "see."

Shamanism is a spirituality of animism. According to this worldview, everything in creation contains its own individual spirit and, therefore, its own innate intelligence. The shaman is fluent in the language of these spirits and is able to communicate in a mutual dialogue with them. In his or her journeys through the Middle World, the shaman is able to connect to, say, the spirit of a rock, a tree, or a hawk, to divine knowledge from the language of the spirits of such things. If a person comes to him or her with an illness, he or she might consult the spirit of a certain plant in order to gather information on the best way to treat the person's specific ailment. Once a person is tuned into it, the world becomes a living, breathing, intelligent entity that communicates constantly in its language of signs and symbols. Viewed in this context, the world ceases to be a place of simple inanimate objects but instead becomes alive with the whispering of the stones and the humming of the trees in their subtle metaphorical language.

This idea of the spirit-in-all-things is explained brilliantly by Machaelle Small Wright in her book, *Behaving as if the God in All Things Mattered*:

> The Carrot Deva (Spirit) "pulls together" the various energies that determine the size, color, texture, growing season, nutritional needs, shape, flower and seed process of the carrot. In essence, the Carrot Deva is responsible for the carrot's entire physical package. It holds the vision of the carrot in perfection, calls together the energies required to formulate that perfection and holds that collection of energies together as it passes from one vibratory level to another on its route to becoming physical. Everything about the carrot on a practical level, as well as on the more expanded, universal level, is known by the Carrot Deva.[14]

Looking at it in this light, it would seem that not only does a carrot have a physical DNA but also a kind of spiritual DNA template, which contains all the properties and characteristics of it, as well as its greatest potential for existence. In the shaman's view of the world, each of these spirits is a reflection of the creative force that exists behind everything in the universe, interweaving strands in the cosmic web that makes up the whole of creation.

Travels into the Middle World can also include connecting to places and times that exist, or have existed, on the physical plane but that may for whatever reason be impossible to access through "ordinary reality."[15] For example, during my Middle World journey in which my consciousness traveled down a physical path in the woods, finding the shell in the clearing, by altering my consciousness in order to attune with that particular location, I was able to step outside of the usual restraints of time and space in order to view something that was not physically accessible at the time. Imagine the possibilities of this! From commonplace uses such as locating a set of lost keys to more urgent requirements such as determining the location of a missing child, the potential is unlimited. Connecting to the physical world in such a way would give us the opportunity to enjoy our world more fully, to not be limited by the usual restrictions that keep us from experiencing the magic and fullness of the world in its totality. Looking at reality through this lens, the world becomes a new place—an explosion of life and light and possibility.

The 4 Directions

Within the Middle World, existing at points around the circumference of the physical plane, are the four cardinal directions of North, South, East, and West. The creation myths of ancient people offer explanations as to the nature of these directions. In Scandinavian mythology, the god Odin, having created the universe from the giant Ymir, set the giant's skull over the earth and called it the sky. At the four quarters, he placed four dwarves named Nordi, Sudri, Austri, and Vestri (or North, South, East, and West).[16] In the Cherokee creation story, Great Spirit fastened the newly formed lands to the sky with four rawhide cords stretching from the four sacred mountains of the four sacred directions.[17] As in these cases, these cardinal points represent the space where the earth and sky join one another. As a glass holds water, the four directions make up the container in which the universe holds its shape.

All earth-honoring spiritual traditions throughout the world that I am aware of consider the directions to be sacred. Sometimes known as the Four Teaching Directions, the Four Winds, or the Four Horizons, the four directions are seen as living spaces that make up a portion of the shaman's pantheon of spirit allies. As are the signs of the zodiac, each of the directions is usually said to reflect and embody an emotional quality, as well as being represented by an animal, color, element, and season. In the Jewish shamanic tradition,[18] in fact, the Hebrew name for each of the directions does not describe a latitude but, rather, an attribute.[19] Much in the same way that a Catholic might appeal to a specific saint (for example, a sailor caught in rough seas may call upon St. Erasmus, the patron saint of mariners) during ritual, the shaman will often invoke the powers of the four directions, inviting them to be present during the ceremony.

As with the descriptions of the three worlds, the classifications and representations given to each direction differ throughout the traditions and change according to each culture's physical and spiritual topography. Still, certain consistencies do exist.

The directions of East and West are easiest to discuss in general terms. Their symbolism is the most obvious and universal, mainly because of their significance as the trajectory of the sun's journey across the sky. East, the place from which the sun arises each morning, is most often seen as the direction identified with beginnings, with rebirth and illumination. Because of this, the East direction is often associated with the season of spring. In the Peruvian tradition, as well as in a great number of Native American traditions, East is represented by large birds and, therefore, the element of air.

As the "land of the setting sun," West is most commonly thought of as the place of endings, of death and darkness and introspection and, therefore, autumn. In at least one tradition that I am aware of, West is the place where the individual faces death in order to move beyond it without fear. Water is the element most frequently ascribed to the West, along with the color blue (although, as with anything else, the color associations may vary significantly from tradition to tradition).

North and South are harder to pin down, though, again, consistencies do appear. In the Jewish kabbalistic tradition, as well as in many Native American philosophies, South is associated with fire, with the color red, with summer, and with growth. The North direction, in contrast, is considered the place of winter, of endurance, and the resting place of ancestors awaiting rebirth.[20]

The attributes associated with each of the four directions can also be looked at as representations of experiences within an individual's life journey. As are the turning of the seasons, our journey through life is cyclical. Moment to moment, day to day, lifetime to lifetime, each of us exists within an unending circle of death, rebirth, growth, and rest. Many traditions represent this process through the Medicine Wheel, a diagram of the great pathway that each of us walks throughout a lifetime as we pass through various stages of evolution and consciousness. In this model, the four directions make up the spokes of the great wheel, with each one a representation of a stage that the individual passes through countless times over the course of a lifetime.

To become disoriented is to return to chaos. An awareness of the four directions, therefore, is fundamental to the shaman's practice not only in terms of his or her physical orientation in space, but as a means of determining the location of his or her spirit allies, as well as the direction on the cosmic wheel that is currently informing one's life at any given moment.

The Great Cosmic Stew

Although such terminology as Middle, Lower, and Upper Worlds suggests a division of each realm of the cosmos, with worlds piled one on top of the other the way layers of a cake are, this labeling is actually an arbitrary process, a way for our linear, compartmentalizing minds to grasp the concepts. In truth, however, these "parts" are no more separate from one another than threads in an ornate tapestry. At some point in the spiritual process, one must cease to think of such things in linear terms. The logical mind must let go of these delineations and erase the boundaries of separation. The challenge, then, is how to do that: how to recondition the mind to grasp such an unfamiliar concept. To try to explain in words is an exercise in futility, as words by their very nature limit us to a set of pre-conceptions. This is where experience, not books or lectures, becomes the greatest teacher. As the Chinese proverb says, "What I hear, I forget. What I see, I remember. What I do, I know."

However, for the purposes of this book, one may think of the universe as a kind of vibrational stew. In a bowl of stew, the carrots take on the flavor of the meat, the meat is marinated by the broth, and the broth contains the essence of all the various flavors and spices added to it. In much the same way, these various levels of vibration flow through and around each other to make up the whole.

Puma Quispe, a native medicine person of the Peruvian tradition, told me:

> The minute we start separating [these three worlds], we start creating blockages. Always they are linked. Always they are interwoven. If we perceive them as separated, or even as levels, then we have blocked the flow of energy and the energies won't flow through. If you are looking at them as separated, in that moment you have created blockages. As long as we realize they are not separated, the blockages disappear. It's something we have to deal with in our hearts.[21]

The Cosmos Within and Without

According to this view of the cosmos, the only thing that separates any of us from the rest of creation is our mind. When that mind is open, the soul of an individual can be seen as a microscopic representation of the rest of creation. The hands and feet, say reflexologists, contain a kind of road map to the rest of our body. Each strand of our DNA, scientists tell us, contains our entire genetic makeup, a reflection of our physical selves. Extend that vision outward and our entire self—spiritual, mental, emotional and physical—becomes a template of the universe. Each of us is a microcosm that reflects and contains the macrocosm (a "small world" version of the greater world) and where one begins and the other ends is nearly impossible to say.

This holographic model of the universe gives us a revolutionary look at the connection between our inner world and the outer worlds, including the three worlds of indigenous cosmology.

Puma Quipse had this to say of the Andean view of the realms:

> [The three worlds] relate to our physical body. When we walk, one step, the other step, there is an energy line that goes from one to the next. We say that is walking the path of the serpent. So our *Ukhupacha* [Lower World] level is from our knees below. From our knees up [the torso] is the energy of the puma, the power of experiencing this world. All of the heavy energy is digested here, just as all of our food is digested here, and the power of our heart is representing the courage of the warrior. All the things that come in this life—whether it is fear, whether it is cold, whether it is heat—everything is experienced here in this area, in the *Kaypacha* [Middle World]—the area of the puma. And then, here, our eyes, our ability to have far vision like the condor, and, like the condor, to live a lifetime, to see a lifetime in one flight. To connect to the condor [the symbol of the *Hanaqpacha*, the Upper World] means we can experience lifetimes.[22]

The connections are vast. We can look at the Hindu system of chakras, which describes the root chakra, located at the base of the spine, as the location where the life force manifests. At the top of the head is the crown chakra, described as the place of mergence with God. We can take Jung's psychological model of the psyche, in which he outlined multiple layers of the unconscious and their archetypes, and see a reflection of the three worlds and the beings that reside there.

Alex Stark, whose shamanic practice includes an eclectic mix of South American curanderismo, Oriental geomancy, and Celtic mysticism, extends this idea one step further. Not only are we a reflection of the universe, Stark told me, but we *are the universe ourselves*:

> This whole journey of life is fundamentally an attempt to remember that at the most intimate personal level we are the center of the world. We are the center of the cosmos. We are light. We are love. We are God. That's basically it. But it takes time, because after the initial period of childhood, you forget it. Everything in society is designed to help you forget it. So you have to remember that process.[23]

What does this mean to any of us on a practical level and, more specifically, to the work of the shaman? It means everything. Imagine this: If the only reality accessible to any of us is the one that we perceive through our own consciousness, then the entire world that surrounds us is nothing more than a creation of our own minds—or, as the eastern mystical traditions would say, an illusion. But unlike those spiritual traditions that perceive this world as illusory and, therefore, dedicate their practices to transcending it, shamanic philosophy uses the flexibility contained within this knowledge to change this self-induced delusion for the better. It is because of his or her abilities to redesign the illusion at will that gives the shaman the ability to heal, to divine knowledge, to predict the future, and to look deep into the past. Think of it: If we contain all worlds, if we *are* the worlds, then we hold within ourselves the answer to every question that has ever been asked or that ever will be asked. We hold the knowledge of lifetimes, and it is in journeying to that state beyond ego—for the ego is dependent upon the illusion for its very existence—that the shaman removes the obstacles to retrieving this knowledge. When the ego mind is silenced, in that moment, the world as we know it ceases to exist. It is in that space that all things become possible. In this space, a cancerous tumor can shrink and disappear within moments. In this space, the shaman can see the location of a missing child. In that space, the shaman can be present at the moment in which a lemur hiccuped in Madagascar, causing an earthquake to occur in Mexico, and stop the momentum of destruction just as it is being born. It is in this place of all-time and no-time, of all-space and no-space, that magic is translated over into the physical world. The space where this happens is known by many names, here called the axis mundi, the center pillar of the world.

The Axis Mundi

Flowing through the center of the three worlds, connecting the four directions, and binding the cosmos together as a great umbilicus is the *axis mundi*, the center pillar of the world. If one imagines the three worlds in a linear manner, stacked up one on top of the other in layers, then the axis mundi could be represented as a pole running through all three. If one thinks of the universe in terms of a cosmic stew, with everything flowing through and between everything else, the axis mundi can be seen as more of an energetic accessing point, a state similar to the transporter machines in the old *Star Trek* episodes. Instead of the physical self-dissolving and reappearing, however, within the axis mundi the ego and spirit selves dissolve out of duality and merge into oneness with the universe.

Says Alex Stark:

> The center pillar is the "All"—your innermost essence, the point of all beginnings, the center of the world, eternity. It is nowhere, the void, the "unmanifest." It

> is the ladder that connects you with the other worlds;
> the smoke hole through which both you and spirit jour-
> ney. It is the crown of your head and your spine through
> which your soul enters and leaves the body.[24]

As a symbol of ascension and descension between three
worlds, the axis mundi is most often depicted as the World
Tree whose roots plunge down deep into the Underworld and
whose branches extend into the farthest reaches of Heaven.
The *Katha Upanishad* of the Hindu tradition describes the
axis mundi as the "eternal asvattha whose roots rise on high
and whose branches grow low. It is pure, the Brahman, what
is called non-Death. All the worlds rest in it." The best-known
World Tree is *Yggdrasil* of the Norse tradition. According to
the myth, the Norse creator god, Odin, hung in agony from
the tree, in voluntary sacrifice, in order to gain knowledge of
the Rune stones, a means of divining the true present state of
things, as well as the future. In the stories of many cultures,
gods, spirits, and souls used the World Tree as a pathway between Heaven and Earth.

Other symbolic interpretations of the axis mundi include
the ladder and the cross. Some see it as the cosmic mountain,
others a pole. According to some, the pillar of fire and the
burning bush of the Christian tradition also symbolize the
axis mundi. The modern mind might think of it as an elevator
made of pure light in which the spirit self can travel to the
other worlds.

In the practices of the Huichol Indians of Mexico, the axis
mundi is called the *Nierica*. Brant Secunda of the Huichol
tradition told me this:

> The Nierica is the doorway, a portal that connects our
> heart and our spirit to the four directions and to the
> Upper Worlds. In the Huichol cosmology there are
> five directions—the fifth direction being the Nierica—
> the sacred center that connects us to the other four.

Don José [Secunda's teacher] explained the Nierica to
me as the sacred face of the Divine; a mirror reflecting
back the knowledge of the ancient ones. When you go
into the Nierica you connect this world to a hidden
world, a place that allows a human being to speak to
the gods.[25]

The caduceus, a symbol of healing comprised of a wand
around which two serpents are intertwined in apparent opposition, has also been regarded as a representation of the axis
mundi and has been said to reflect the balance and polarity of
the cosmic stream—two opposites merging into one. The caduceus is a particularly apt symbol, as it is within the axis
mundi that the shaman steps into a place where all duality is
dissolved. The journey of the shaman is a journey into the
infinite, into singularity with spirit, and it is here that the
shaman retrieves the knowledge as to how best bring the worlds
of flesh and spirit into harmony and therefore bring healing
to the physical world. Through ceremonies, through experiences in other worlds, the shaman—or any individual who
establishes a close connection to spirit—is able to reconnect
the physical to the sacred, thus establishing an equilibrium
between the two.

The Christian myth of the rise and fall of the Tower of
Babel is a good allegorical representation of what happens when
a society relies solely on the physical as a means of accessing
God. As the story goes, the Tower of Babel was built as a gateway to Heaven, intended to artificially restore the broken primordial axis and create a means to ascend to the world of God.
Because the Tower had been artificially created, it produced
confusion on both earthly and divine levels. God, therefore,
destroyed the Tower and scattered the human race across the
world. According to *The Penguin Dictionary of Symbols*, "Human beings no longer understood one another and no longer
spoke the same language, that is to say that there was no
longer the slightest consensus between them, each individual

proclaiming himself or herself absolute and alone."[26] The word *Babel* itself is derived from the root *Bll*, meaning "to confound." The role of the shaman within this cosmological framework, then, is to act as an intermediary between the physical world and the levels of spirit, as a balancing point between the two. Without that, we as a people are left with a deep hole inside us that needs to be filled. We have the sensation that something is missing and try to fill the lack with material goods and achievements. Unfortunately, such "answers" are only temporary stopgaps and come with the steep price of environmental degradation, rampant violence, and an epidemic level of depression among our people.

*   *   *

The cosmology of the shaman can be taken in any context that makes sense to the seeker. These worlds can be described as distant realms, parallel universes, states of mind, levels of energetic vibration, or a reflection of the collective unconscious. No matter what terms one relates to them, however, one must never lose sight of the fact that these are realms and processes that exist *both within the self and beyond the self.* Too often we take the axiom "as within, so without" and get stuck in one or the other side of the equation. For example, one can legitimately compare the Lower, Middle, and Upper Worlds to the subconscious, conscious, and superconscious as a way of relating to it therapeutically. The danger in this, however, is getting stuck in this mode of perception, thereby limiting oneself to seeing it only as an internal process.

Although viewing the worlds psychologically is certainly a good and valuable tool for exploring the reaches of inner space, in times of reverence and in times of need, one must call upon that which exists beyond personal psychology, that which is greater than the small self. Understand a spiritual process in psychological terms if need be, but don't stay stuck in one perspective of it. Extend that understanding outward to something greater than the self. In the same way, one can get stuck focusing only on the macro, on Spirit, and remove oneself from the equation. As you read this book, try hard not to limit yourself to just one mode of thinking about it, but allow it to be a three-dimensional experience. One of the greatest gifts of the shaman is the ability to hold many truths at once, knowing that all things are connected, and all things in their simplicity reflect the greater whole. Whatever their nature, exploration of these worlds is of vital significance to one following the shamanic path. Each of us holds the imprint of the entire universe within us, and each of us has the potential to have a one-to-one experience with Creation. In this way, we become co-creators with the forces of nature, with the spirits, and, ultimately, with the Creator itself.

In the chapters that follow, it will be important to keep in mind the cosmological framework that births such ideas, placing the individual as a reflection of Spirit.

Exercises

The purpose behind the exercises in this chapter is to establish a mode of resonance and a heartfelt connection to the cosmic structure. Their aim is to help you become comfortable acting within the cosmic sphere, the landscape of the cosmos that both surrounds you and that is you.

Before jumping into this first set of exercises, however, I would like to take a moment to discuss the exercises that appear throughout this book and, specifically, how one can get the most out of them.

Although connecting to one's spirit mind or spirit consciousness may seem like a daunting task, most spiritual exercises are incredibly simple. This simplicity may be deceptive. It may seem as though nothing very "magical" is happening to you as you do them, but don't be fooled by your logical mind. These exercises can open up a door in your consciousness if you allow yourself to go fully into them. Any kind of shift in consciousness does—and should—take time, practice, and patience. Many of the shifts you experience will be subtle, others more visceral. Therefore, my suggestion is that you first read the book in its entirety. When you are done, go back through each set of exercises, taking as much time as you need in order to feel comfortable and solid with them before moving on to the next. Also, as each set of exercises lays the groundwork for the next, I recommend sticking to the order that they are presented here in the book. This is an example of where working without a teacher can be difficult, for it sometimes takes an outside observer to know when the student is ready for the next step. However, for the purposes of this book, you must let your own inner guidance be your mentor as well as the input of any other person that you may be sharing these experiences with. Take it slowly. Remember: Any path to mastery takes a lifetime or more to achieve. There is strength in small steps. Try to step out of a goal-oriented frame of mind when doing these. The purpose of a spiritual exercise is not to achieve some end result. Approach it the way you approach taking a bath: The purpose of taking a bath is usually not to get clean, but to simply be in the space. In that same way, with these exercises it is the journey, the process of transformation from one thing to another, that really counts. As you practice these exercises, remember to be loving and gentle with yourself, for to be loving is to be fully connected to the world. The moment fear or self-doubt descends on us we close ourselves off from our greatest potential. Let go of all preconceived notions of what is "right" and "wrong." These labels serve no purpose but to limit.

Many of these exercises involve doing a lot of writing, so it is recommended that you purchase a journal in which to write or, if you prefer, use a tape recorder to record your experiences. I, personally, chose writing because it is the medium that feels most comfortable to me. However, as this work is all about individual expression, I encourage others to use whatever creative interpretation you feel most connected to engage with your experience. This may include dancing, singing, painting, running—the options are limitless.

Before each exercise, it is important that you prepare yourself and your personal space. Disconnect the phone, change into comfortable clothes, light incense—anything that helps you to connect to your own inner awareness with as few distractions as possible. Always purify yourself first. This can include taking a bath or smudging oneself with the smoke from a fire or a bundle of sage. Then, find a position, either sitting or standing, that feels comfortable to you. Focus on your breathing so that your breaths in and out are smooth and unobstructed. (A slow humming or chanting can be helpful in focusing the breath.) Imagine each inhale as imbuing you with power and wisdom and each exhale as an opportunity to expel any old, stale belief systems that are no longer useful to you. As you exhale, take any emotional or physical distractions that you may have and send them out of and away from you.

Next, set your intent for the exercise—for example, what it is you hope to achieve by doing it. Speak an affirmation out loud or to yourself, such as, "My intent is to [learn more about myself, feel at one with the cosmos, fill in the blank]." Ask for guidance and support from all your allies, both known and unknown to you. Then begin.

Throughout each exercise I will remind you to repeat this process by telling you to "prepare yourself and your space." These steps are vital and must not be passed over half-heartedly. Purification and relaxation are key to both success and safety in this work. They create a space where the results can show up, a way to open the door and step over the threshold into sacred relationship with the cosmos. Once you have finished with the exercise, be sure to give thanks to your allies for each teaching you have received. As in any relationship, a sense of appreciation and gratitude and reverence will keep the energy flowing back and forth in a mutual exchange. Finally, ground yourself using the method described in the final exercise of this chapter or another that you are familiar with. Grounding is essential. In fact, one could argue that the most important part of the shaman's experience is his or her return to the physical world. Shamanism is about connection with the earth as well as the heavens. Without this return, and the bringing back of gifts of knowledge and power, the shaman's experiences are of very little use to his or her community.

Exercise #1: The Center Pillar Exercise

This exercise is an oldie but a goodie. In 1938, Israel Regardie first published a version of this exercise in his book *The Middle Pillar*. Since then it has been a staple training for all such work. Each version of the Center Pillar Exercise varies slightly, depending on who is explaining it, though the basic form remains the same. (The version I've included here is the version that I use, as it was explained to me by my teachers.)

One of my teachers insists that most people will never get anywhere in this work without practicing this exercise, which makes sense. The center pillar is the gateway to all other worlds, and therefore the ability to access it is vital. Without getting too bogged down in expectation, allow yourself to explore the feelings that you have within this space. See what comes up the more you practice. Do not discount even the subtlest sensation or experience.

Prepare yourself and your space as illustrated previously. Sit, stand, or lay in a comfortable position. Breathe intentionally. After a few moments, imagine a beam of pure, radiant white light entering the crown of your head. Feel its warmth as it continues to flow through you, all the way down your spinal cord and into the ground beneath you. Imagine the light radiating through you, dissolving any negativity or ego concerns you may have, until you become a pure channel.

Take your time. What sensations come to you? Experience and explore the feeling for as long as you wish, offer thanks, and then write about your experiences in your journal. Know that the center pillar is within you at all times. In the beginning you may have to practice in order to strengthen your connection to it. Whenever you have a moment throughout the day, especially at moments when you are in need of clarity, stop and reconnect yourself to the center pillar.

Exercise #2: Middle World Attunement

Taking the time to get to know the Middle World, the world of everyday, physical existence, is one of the most gratifying experiences one can have on this path. Too often as spiritual seekers we try to escape from what we see as the world of mundane existence, looking for the magic that exists "out there." In fact, the world around us contains more magic than we will ever be aware of when we engage with it in an ordinary mode of consciousness. Sacred land is the spot on which you stand. There are an infinite number of exercises that one can do to access this magic and energy. This is one.

Explore the natural world; get to know its wisdom. Shamans are the ultimate observers, and being in tune with nature and its rhythms is the foundation for their work. Find a spot in the natural world that calls to you. Spend some time there each day. After going into your preparation technique, observe the landscape around you using all of your senses. What sounds do you hear from the wind, from the birds? How does the earth smell? Go into the consciousness of a child and enter into a dialogue with a stone, a tree. Ask it simple questions and wait for the answers to come. Do be aware, as one of my teachers was constantly reminding us, that the tree will not grow lips and say, "Have a nice day!" This kind of conversation is done psychically—made up of images and symbols instead of words—and is a different·kind of "listening" from the one that we normally engage with.

Again, "take a bath" in the moment. Don't rush or focus on a goal. Imagine you are getting to know your lover's body. With the deepest appreciation, open all your senses, giving every sensation your fullest attention. Write down your impressions. Notice how the place responds differently to you once you have been coming there for a long time. Offer thanks.

Exercise #3: Designing Your Own Landscape

This exercise is a warm-up to the Shamanic Journey Exercise that you will be taken through in a later chapter. In it you will be "designing your own landscape"—that is, establishing a personalized landscape of the three worlds from which you can begin your exploration. Although some people can easily move right into a journey without this exercise, others may benefit from warming up on this exercise. I, personally, found that my actual journeys were much more vivid and useful once I had a little practice in "teaching my mind how to misbehave" (to quote Stephen King). Have fun with this. Remember that there is no right or wrong answer. This is your landscape to design, as you desire. Nothing is fixed; the landscape can always change if you desire it to.

Prepare yourself and your space. Feel yourself within the center pillar. Now, focus your attention on thoughts of the Lower World. What does the Lower World feel like? What does it look like? What sensory impressions of taste, touch, sight, sound, and smell do you get when your awareness is attuned to it? Engage with all your senses. What do you see? Perhaps your "seeing" is not clear but you have a feeling. Are there sounds? What can you touch, and what touches you? Experience this world with a child's mind.

Either as you are doing this or immediately afterward, record your impressions. Look them over after you have done so. Which of your impressions do you feel come from an outward source, such as the religion of your upbringing, what you have been told at school, by your parents, or even by something that I have written in this book? Which are your own authentic impressions? Feel free to discard anything you feel is inauthentic to your own experience and keep the rest. Do remember, however, that these outward sources may hold truth for you as well. Many shamans, for example, use the Christ energy in their work. It may take time to discern what works for you and what doesn't, so be careful not to discount anything too quickly. If you wish, you could dance your impressions of the Lower World, make a poem out of it, create a song out of it, or paint a painting that represents it.

Repeat this exercise, this time turning your attention to the Upper World and doing the same. Always offer thanks.

Exercise #4: Dowsing the 4 Directions

Go to a place outdoors where you can sit or stand comfortably. Prepare yourself and your space. Using a compass, position yourself facing South. Still your mind, breathe, and place yourself within the center pillar. Then, take note of all the thoughts, feelings, visualizations, and sensations that pass through your mind or come into your body. When you are done, jot down your impressions and turn and face the West. Do the same for the West. Then turn to the North and do the same. Then the East. Practice this exercise in different locations. When you feel you are ready, go to a new place and, without looking at the compass this time, try to determine which direction you are facing using only your senses. Try to do this at noon when the sun is at its midpoint in the sky or after dark so that the sun is not giving you any hints! You may sense nothing at first. As with all exercises, be patient, be loving to yourself, and stick with it. Give thanks.

Exercise #5: Grounding

Practicing these exercises may leave you in a very altered state. Before going on to the next one, or just returning to life as usual, you will need to "come back to earth." When I first began this path, I was stubborn and didn't want to ground in between exercises because, as I reasoned, if I stayed in the elevated space I was in after the first exercise, I would go into an even higher state if I went directly into the next. Wrong! That tactic just left me feeling disconnected. My exercises lacked grounding and made me feel like a balloon that was being dragged haphazardly around by the wind. I came to understand that all this was like being on a trampoline: The further back down to earth you go, the greater "liftoff" you get as you go into the next exercise.

Cheryl Krisko, an incredibly talented energy worker, gave the following grounding exercise to me and graciously allowed me to use it here:

"Sit in a chair with your knees apart and your feet resting solidly on the ground. Your hands may rest gently on your knees. Do not rush, but find a comfortable pace and begin to breathe in and out, gently filling your belly first, and then your lungs. Slowly exhale. As you breathe, imagine that the breath comes in through your right foot and flows up the right side of your body to the top of your head. As you exhale, feel the air travel down the left side of your body and out your left foot. Notice any areas in your body where the flow might feel restricted or uneven. Continue to breathe up the right side and down the left, gently and at your own pace until you feel a nice flow of energy in your body.

"Now begin to breathe up the back of your body—up the back of both legs, up the spine and the back of the head. Breathe out, feeling the breath flow over your face, down your chest and abdomen, and into the front of the legs and back to the earth. Continue as long as you wish, but do not rush. Six breaths may do the trick, or do as many as you like.

"Once you have done the circulations to your comfort and satisfaction, continue to sit in the same position with eyes closed and gently notice your body on the inside. When you feel ready, begin to send roots down into the earth from your tailbone, which is resting on the seat of the chair. Feel the roots begin to travel downward—maybe through several stories of the building below you—and touch the surface of the earth. Can you tell what the ground is like? Gently continue to stretch your roots to the earth beneath you. Allow them to expand, and as they continue to grow into the earth, begin to feel the flow of earthly energies into your own being. Sit with this connection and, when ready, give thanks and gently open your eyes, leaving your connection intact."

Chapter 2

Embracing the Shadow, Illuminating the Divine: The Shaman's Initiation Ordeal

At birth, we come into this world in perfect spiritual unity with the universe around us. In those first moments of existence, we are still aware of ourselves as part of a greater whole, with no boundaries between this and that, self and other. Starting with a biological and identity connection to mother and extending outward, the infant sees everything that exists as an extension of his or her being.

These precious moments do not last long. As early as two to six months, a dim awareness of the rest of the world as separate, as "other," begins to emerge. By 15 months of age, infants learn to perceive themselves as separate from mother, from other people and things. Every moment after the first breath is taken is devoted to rooting ourselves in the physical. This transition is an essential part of our survival in the material realm. We learn to attend to each of our bodily needs as they occur in the instant, not least of which is the desire for love, which, to the infant who must rely on the acceptance of "other" to fulfill its needs, is synonymous with survival and self-preservation. Thus begins our gradual transformation from a unified consciousness to the development of the ego as the center of conscious awareness.

As he or she grows, the child's self concept grows with him or her, changing and developing to come into alignment with the dictates of tribe, family, and society. Even as adults, this sense of ourselves as separate and distinct individuals is essential to our survival in the physical world. It is because of our ego, our "I" awareness, that we can get ourselves dressed in the morning, cross the street safely, fly to the moon. Unfortunately, having been given too much control over the psyche, the ego mind (some call this the "left brain") quickly becomes the spoiled child of the psyche, bound and determined to keep us focused on the part of the self that defines who we are as individuals, thereby separating us from the rest of creation. Unlike the newborn's view of all things being connected and interdependent, the ego mind sees the rest of the world as being in opposition to the self. By this I do not mean *in conflict* exactly; rather, it sees the rest of creation as a point of comparison to the "I." As in, "You are tall; I am short." "This is inanimate, whereas I breathe and move." The ego mind believes in absolutes. It cringes at ambiguity, at paradox, at non-duality, and at the illogical—in short, anything else that threatens its tight grip on the psyche.

As is the string that holds a balloon tied to its tether, the function of the ego self is to root us in the physical plane, all of which is in opposition to the shaman's ultimate goal as mediator between the physical and spiritual planes. The fundamental philosophical principle of shamanism is the belief that all things are connected, that, at the most basic level, there is no difference between me and you, the computer on which I type, and the half-eaten apple that sits, growing brown, on the corner of my desk. It is this unity consciousness that gives the shaman his or her power, for, as we have seen in the previous chapter and will continue to discuss from here on out, once the boundaries of separation have been lowered, one's potential for movement across the universe—and for action within the physical plane—becomes limitless.

In order to engage in this reconciliation between Heaven and Earth, the shaman must learn to step outside of the rational, ego-rooted mind and to transfer consciousness into a state of divine union. This is an excruciatingly difficult process, for the ego mind, in its terror of being annihilated, will hang on tooth and nail for control. To become a shaman therefore involves a radical transformation of consciousness, a kind of temporary exorcism of the ego, which will allow the shaman to drop the "I" state and make the switch from the conscious to the unconscious, from the logical to the intuitive, from the ego mind to the spirit mind into which he or she will be traveling. This is not to say that the ego must be destroyed entirely for, as we have seen, the ego is a vital part of our experience on the physical plane. The ego mind is, however, a tyrant and does not like to share power. In order for the shaman to be successful on his or her path, he or she must learn to release the tight grip of the ego during the duration of the shaman's magical flights.

In order for this transformation to occur, the neophyte shaman must undergo the ancient rite of initiation in which the he or she is violently and traumatically propelled, either willingly or unwillingly, past the boundaries of the self into a state a divine union with cosmos and creation.

The 5 Stages of Mergence

Every shamanic culture around the world has its own specific types of initiation practices and methods. An exploration of just one of them would take an entire book. However, as with the descriptions of the three worlds, the underlying rhythm of the initiation process remains remarkably consistent from tradition to tradition. Instead of detailing the specific rituals as they are practiced in each individual culture, I will focus on the recurring themes that pop up in relation to initiation practices across the world and how they provide a means of spiritual transformation to the shamanic candidate.

It is, of course, impossible to compartmentalize this experience into neat little boxes. These stages of initiation often overlap and interchange, repeat themselves in some cases, and jump ahead in others. In general, however, the initiate's movement of consciousness towards this state of union can be sorted into five distinct stages:

1. Calling/Awakening.
2. Purification/Purgation.
3. Revelation.
4. Worldly Return.
5. Spiritual Renewal.[1]

Each of these stages represents levels of psycho-spiritual growth that the shaman must pass through in order to alter the rhythm of his or her consciousness. Likened to the skin of an onion, each represents a layer, a veil of consciousness that must be peeled away piece by piece, in order to reach the place of purity, understanding, and, finally, mergence with Spirit. Within this process the candidate oscillates between light and darkness, exultation and sorrow, the ecstasy of complete mergence and the anguish of utter abandonment. It is a dangerous task—both physically and mentally—and one without any guarantee of accomplishment. If successful, the candidate will experience a death of his or her self as it is interpreted solely by the ego mind, followed by a rebirth into oneness with the unified mind of the cosmos. If not, he or she may be lost to the process—forever stuck in one of these stages, often manifesting itself as a mental, emotional, or physical illness. Because of the importance of total transformation, in many traditions, the elders of the community do not consider the candidate a true shaman until he has successfully navigated his way through each of these stages at least once. The powerful shaman knows that he or she will cycle through these stages again and again, constantly undergoing a process of growth to achieve a new level of understanding and power.

This transformation is an arduous psychological and spiritual process, filled with both physical and psychological trials and suffering geared towards shattering, then redesigning, the neophyte's sense of self. The initiatory journey is an experience of self-exploration for the shaman as well as an exploration of the universe at large. For, as we are coming to understand, to know the inner workings of oneself is to know the outer workings of the cosmos.

The Calling/Awakening

The journey of a thousand miles begins with a single step. This first step of the shaman's initiatory journey is the "Calling" or "Awakening" phase and is marked by the initiate's first experience crossing over into the spiritual realm. This is the moment of revelation for the neophyte, his or her first glimpse into non-ordinary reality and the powers and possibilities that reside there. As in the initial stage of Joseph Campbell's shaman's journey, this is the hero's call to arms, the moment in which latent talents and abilities are awakened and a new purpose for the self—in this case, one involving a life of service to his or her community—is proposed.

In general, there are two ways in which the potential shaman can be "called." Most dramatically, the Awakening comes about as a kind of recruitment by the spirits who make their wishes known by thrusting the initiate into a new perceptual state, out of ego mind and into infinite oneness. Others come to the path of their own volition or are guided to the path by elders who see inherent abilities within the individual, and seek out this ego-less state through a variety of means.

Recruitment by the Spirits

Recruitment by the spirits can be a terrifying ordeal for the one chosen to undertake the Calling. This manner of Awakening is most often brought about by a sudden physical and/or mental illness that radically transforms the candidate's consciousness into a state of sudden and unintentional mergence with the spirit world. There is a good reason for this. Whereas a healthy person is likely to filter divine messages to alter it to his personality, the dying and "insane" have radically altered psyches that may be able to better accept the information and experience in its purity. Because of this, the initiate, whether the entrance onto the path of shamanism is intentional or experienced as a "spiritual abduction," must "lose his or her mind" in order to readjust his mental reception to the frequency of the spirit world.

As was the case with Black Elk in his initiatory journey, one way in which the spirits transport the shaman into nonordinary reality is by way of a physical sickness. Initiation stories from around the world are filled with accounts of "shamanic illnesses," in which the potential shaman falls into a state close to death, or even into death itself, and, during this breakdown of consciousness, is transported to the invisible realms. In this way, the physical sickness of the shaman becomes a teaching in itself, for the shaman must cross over to the place beyond death where he or she will one day have to follow his or her clients. The *Sakha* people of Siberia believe the shaman can cure only those diseases whose spirits have tasted the shaman during initiation.[2] In this way the shaman follows the journey of the "wounded healer," learning to heal himself before he can heal another.

Oscar Miro-Quesada is a shaman of the Peruvian *curandero* tradition. As a child, he suffered from recurring bouts of severe asthma. At age 10, he experienced an attack so acute that he felt himself leaving the physical plane. In this altered state of consciousness, he recalls, "Three very wizen old beings called me back and told me a lot of things about where I came from and where I was heading to. After that I was healed and never had asthma again."[3] Years later as a teenager, with the experience long forgotten in favor of the more mundane concerns of adolescence, Miro-Quesada traveled to the northern coast of Peru to find don Celso Rojas, a curandero who was reported to be the best San Pedro[4] maker in the world. During a San Pedro ceremony with don Celso, the same three old men rose out of don Celso's altar and reminded him of everything they had told him regarding his future: the marriage he was going to have, the schools that he would go to, the children he would have. Based on that awakening experience, he began an apprenticeship with don Celso that continued for many years.

In other cases of spiritual recruitment, the future shaman may remain physically healthy but begin to exhibit behavior that in ordinary reality seems nonsensical and "out of touch." The person may begin to act in a strange manner; babbling gibberish; having hallucinations; hearing voices; or even simply showing signs of being listless, depressed, or otherwise "removed" from and unable to function in daily life. What we in modern culture would consider a mental illness is, in some cases, actually a vocational crisis—an indication that the spirits are calling a man or woman to follow the path of the shaman. Mircea Eliade observed that "among many tales of shamanic initiation, he or she who was destined to become a prophet-priest suddenly disappears, carried off by the spirits (often into the sky) returning some days or weeks later, often into a state of madness."[5]

As with those having undergone initiation via a physical illness, the inner experience of the individual undergoing this kind of calling is quite different from what it looks like to those around him. Although from the vantagepoint of consensual reality the individual has not physically "gone" anywhere, the visionary experience of the candidate is one of being kid-napped by the spirits and brought to a place outside of ordinary reality. These experiences can involve travels to the Upper or Lower Worlds as well as a "dismembering" and subsequent reassembling of the shaman's body so that it will be new and fresh and strong and ready to receive and hold powerful teachings within it. In this state, the neophyte undergoes a violent dismemberment followed by a rebuilding and a transmission of power and subsequent initiation with spirit guides and teachers.

There are remarkable similarities the world over to describe this process of mental abduction of the initiate by the spirits. In the Celtic tradition, those who exhibit certain kinds of abnormal behavior are often referred to as being "taken by the fairies."[6] In the Tibetan Bon shamanic tradition, future shamans are said to be abducted by the *ban jhankri*, a yeti-like creature that captures young candidates and brings them back to its cave in order to initiate them into shamanism. Those who are *chako*, or pure of heart and body, remain with the ban jhankri for teaching and transferal of power. Those that are not are ravaged and tossed out.[7] Islamic and pre-Islamic lore refers to the "inspired madmen" known as the *Kahins* or Oracle-mongers. These were men who had their wits taken away by *djinns*—elemental spirits—and who lived in the valleys and deserts of Arabia, uttering prophesies to those willing to listen.[8] In central Africa, legends exist about a "half man" who challenges those who encounter him to fight. If defeated, the half man trades the knowledge of healing in exchange for his life and the lucky victor becomes a proficient medicine person. If not, the loser faces an unpleasant death.[9]

Although we in the western world may not have a culturally accepted tradition that explains these experiences in such a mystical light, it is likely, if not certain, that this kind of calling occurs here as well. Unfortunately, in modern culture, such states carry with them not socio-spiritual significance, but shame and isolation. Those who experience this kind of calling in the west tend to do so without the aid of elders to put the crisis in perspective and guide the individual through the process. Without this aid, the potential shaman may risk becoming stuck in a disjointed visionary state, in which the visions control the initiate rather than the other way around.

Oscar Miro-Quesada told me:

> As a clinician myself, I have found that about seventy percent of all socio-psychotic experiences are spiritual emergencies. The other thirty percent are psychopathological illnesses. But in the rest of these cases, if you help the client or the patient interpret his or her experiences as a spiritual awakening rather than a sickness, they find purpose and meaning in the experience rather than condemnation by societal norms.... If they had a community of like-hearted souls to offer nurturance for their shamanic initiation to run its course, seventy percent of Western psychopathology could be shapeshifted into a spiritual awakening.[10]

Refusing the Call

These sudden encounters with non-ordinary reality are intentionally shattering to the candidate's view of reality. Through these experiences, the initiate's mind is expanded to encompass all realities that exist—not just those within the reach of the five physical senses. During the Calling phase of the initiation—and, indeed, each time he makes a trip into the other worlds—the shaman must face death. This death is both symbolic and actual and is one that will rip the shaman's ideas of self and reality into shreds over and over again throughout the course of the initiation and of his life.

Knowing the psychological sacrifices he or she will have to make, many refuse the call to become a shaman for years until it becomes clear that, in these matters, spirit gives very little choice. Those who refuse this call are often called again—

and again and again and again, each time in ways that are more traumatizing and harder and harder for the candidate to ignore.

Some are dragged kicking and screaming onto the path. In his book *Native Healer*, Medicine Grizzlybear Lake recounts his own call to service, which came in the form of several near-death experiences throughout his early life. Despite the obvious calling, the life of the shaman was not one that he entered willingly:

> I didn't want to be a native healer—I was chosen for it. Four different times in my life I went to elderly medicine people in the Indian way and asked them to take it out of me. I gave them a lot of money, gifts, and even offered hard labor to have the power taken away. I didn't want the responsibility, hardship, sacrifice, and strict life that went with it. Two of these Elders refused. One tried to do what I asked and died exactly a year later. The fourth one, Rolling Thunder, really scolded me. He said: "This is not your choosing. You don't have the right or authority to interfere with what the Great Spirit has decided. You were chosen to be a medicine man long before you came into this body on this Earth. You have a duty and the responsibility to follow the calling. If not, you will hurt your family, your people, and the spiritual function and design of the Universe."[11]

The "Inner-Directed" Shaman

Despite the hardships and suffering, there are still those who not only go willingly into the path of shaman, but also seek it out on their own. These are often individuals who feel compelled to enter into the practice of shamanism by an internal bidding. In these cases, the candidate is prompted to seek out and attain this ego-less and boundary-less state by an inner "knowing" that he or she has not yet grasped the fullest extent of the universe and a deep desire to connect with it no matter what the dangers or costs. Some of these people posses a natural tendency to enter such states and go there with ease; others require more discipline and perseverance and training from elder shamans who are willing to teach them.

Sometimes, the individual's desire for this knowledge is enough to turn the attention of the spirits. In 1970, the day after his high school graduation, Brant Secunda left his parents' house in Brooklyn, New York, and made his way down to Ixtlan, Mexico, on a quest to find don Juan, the shaman made famous by the books of Carlos Castaneda. Once in Ixtlan, he learned of a village a five-day walk away. There, he was told, he could meet and study with a shaman. On the third day of his walk into the mountains, Secunda wandered down a deer trail and became lost and disoriented, eventually passing out from dehydration and sun exposure. As he recalled:

> The next thing I knew, I was having these visions of circles of light surrounding me. Inside the circles were all kinds of birds and animals—tigers, pumas, like that. In the very middle was a deer. I was dying, and all the animal powers were there to help me feel my connection to creation.[12]

Not long after he was awakened by a group of Indians standing over him. As it turned out, the Indians were Huichols, part of a small tribe said to be the last people in North America to have maintained their pre-Columbian ways. Eventually, Secunda became an apprentice to don José Matsuwa, one of the tribe's most respected shamans.

In cases in which there has been no previous spiritual recruitment, the initiate may jump ahead to the purification stage, hoping to intentionally seek out this ego-less state through self-induced physical and mental hardship. This takes great faith and persistence by those who do not have it forced upon them by spiritual recruitment, for the ego mind desires to hold on to its comfortable, rational view of the world and does not go quietly. Here, the potential shaman "cries for a vision" or otherwise forces himself into a unitive state by intentional stimuli such as ingesting hallucinogenic plants or drugs, long periods of fasting, ceremony, and other trance-inducing stimuli. In these cases, the shaman-in-training will seek out a teacher in the physical realm with whom he or she will train. This is a fairly typical method of introduction for seekers in the western world, although it occurs in more traditional settings as well. In the Tibetan Bon tradition, if it has not already happened spontaneously, the disciple goes through an initiation with a guru in which he or she calls upon a spirit to possess him or her. Once that occurs, a ritual is held in which the possessing spirit is honored and asked by the guru to become the disciple's tutelary deity. These shamans are often not as respected as those who gain power spontaneously from the spirit world are, however. In the Bon tradition it is said that during the Golden Age, all shamans were *aph se aph* or *rang shin* (spontaneously called). Nowadays, during this *Kaliyuga* or Dark Age, it is said that the connection to heaven is veiled, and, as a result, most shamans have to learn from each other. Many Nepalese shamans believe that the scarcity of *aph se aph* shamans indicates that shamans are becoming less powerful.[13]

Others disagree. When asked how far someone taught in this way can go with this work, Oscar Miro-Quesada responded:

> As far as they want to go. Really, the furthest we'll ever have to travel is from our heads to our hearts. If people start down this path using just their head, it can take a lifetime. *Two* lifetimes. *Three* lifetimes. *Four* lifetimes. But if people wake up to this path with their heart, they don't need to study with any teacher.... Ultimately, prayer is just as powerful. If there is heart in a person's

calling and path, it makes no difference. They are already there.[14]

Purgation/Purification

The Calling stage of the initiation process is the neophyte shaman's first experience crossing over the threshold of the physical into the world of spirit. As we have seen, this baptism is often unintentional on the part of the individual and thereby out of his or her control. If he or she is going to be of any future use to his or her community in the role of shaman, however, it is essential that the initiate learn to journey into these worlds consciously and purposefully. The rest of the initiation therefore involves learning how to reenter the same state of being that he or she was thrust into during the Calling phase, but now learn to do it deliberately and with clear, premeditated intent.

Much like in the Calling phase, the "Purgation/Purification" stage further disintegrates the shaman's sense of self. This is the place of tests and challenges where the shaman must intentionally let go of anything that keeps him or her bound to the physical world, preventing him or her from flying freely into the spirit realm. This phase of the training often requires a number of physical and psychological tests and trials that take a toll on the initiate's mind and body. These include fasting, long periods of isolation, and/or physically demanding pilgrimages to places of power. Food, water, rest—those things that are fundamental to his body's existence—and egoistic attachments are put to the side for a period of time. This self-deprivation is essential for a number of reasons. First of all, it acts as a sign of good faith to the spirits that the initiate is serious and willing to suffer and make some sacrifice in exchange for knowledge. (One is reminded of the Norse myth of Odin hanging upside down from the Tree of Knowledge in self-sacrifice in order to gain wisdom over the Runes.) Secondly, abstaining from those carnal needs such as food, sex, and other distractions cleanses the initiate's mind, body, and spirit, creating a clear channel for the forces of Spirit to act through. In some traditions it is believed that the more pain and suffering the initiate takes upon him or herself during the initiation, the greater his or her powers will be as a shaman.

The Purgation/Purification phase often involves a physical separation from the community, a period in which the initiate leaves the comforts and security of home and goes off into the wilderness alone. With this gesture of intent, the initiate both literally and symbolically returns to the womb of the earth in order to be reborn into a new form. During this process, the initiate retreats from the noise and chatter of the external world to an internal one where he or she must face both the torments of the wilderness as well as those of his or her own soul. It is here in this place of silence that the shaman turns his or her attention inward and begins the process of self-discovery.

Just as this phase cleanses and purifies the body, the shaman must acknowledge and reconcile the part of himself that Jung called the "shadow" self—those fears and limitations that remain hidden from the outside world and, often, from the individual most of all. Left alone to the silence and deprived of the comforts of home, all the initiate's heroic myths about him or herself fall apart like a house of cards as the repressed forces of the unconscious arise to confront him or her. More often than not, the individual discovers hidden parts of the psyche that he or she might wish to remain hidden. In the realm of the shadow, the strong are confronted with their weaknesses, the brave with their timidity, and the loving and merciful with their equal propensity towards hatred and brutality. As painful as it is, this process of self-discovery is of utmost importance to the shaman-in-training, as it brings to light the individual's dual ability to both harm and heal, as well as his or her potential to desire for power over knowledge. Without acknowledging the darker impulses that motivate him, the shaman cannot separate himself from them and, in turn, cannot act as a pure channel for the forces of the universe to work through. Left unaware and out of control, it can cause great damage both to the shaman and to others.

As with the ego, this does not mean that the shaman has to, can, or even should eliminate his shadow entirely. That is impossible. It is also undesirable. The shadow side is one half of the self and is therefore part of what shapes the shaman's power. Light without shadow is a formless mass, unable to contain anything. In a still-life painting, the shape and characteristics of an object are not only determined by the light, but also by the shadow that defines its outer boundaries. In this same way, this shadow side defines the individual. Instead of denying that darkness, the shaman must become conscious of its power and, through ritual and prayer, transform it into liberating energy to be used for healing and service.

A symbolic representation of this idea can be seen in the mesas of the Peruvian north coastal *curanderos*. The *mesa* is an altar upon which the medicine person places his or her power objects and ceremonial tools. The placement of each object is purposeful, and the mesa becomes a kind of map of the unseen worlds, depicting the inner and outer cosmos on its surface. This kind of mesa is divided into three sections. The right side is called the *Campo Justiciero*, the Field of Justice. This is the path of the mystic and holds sacred objects symbolizing Divine Will. The left, called *Campo Ganadero*, or Field of Will, is the place of free will and manipulation, of forcing one's individual desires over what is already present through God, the path of the magician. The place in the middle where these two forces overlap and merge is called *Campo Medio*, the Middle Field, the path of healing. It is by learning to navigate and use each of the three fields and their corresponding energies that the shaman is able to bring benevolent change to the physical world.

For the shaman, coming to know his shadow side goes well beyond just the psychological implications. In the shamanic way of thinking, this shadow, the "demons" of the psyche, are both psychological and actual—that is, they not only represent internal frames of mind but also actual entities that exist within the larger framework of the cosmos and that are responsible for causing imbalance both within the individual and within the world at large. In the Tibetan tradition of Bon shamanism, this "shadow" part of the self represents one of several souls residing within each individual. If a person dies from an unnatural death or does not have an appropriate funeral, this soul becomes a *lha gra*, evil spirit.[15] In this way, the shadow is not just a personal hindrance, but, after death, it becomes a part of the collective experience for the community as well. In learning about his own weaknesses, the shaman gains control over those malicious entities that feed upon the darkness and that will cause illness and suffering in the shaman's future patients. The shaman is also better protected from sorcerers[16] who wish to do psychological or physical harm.

Finding this balance between the extremes of personal will and surrender to divine will is the challenge of the shaman. Over the course of the initiation and, indeed, over the course of a lifetime, the shaman will have to struggle with those two parts of him or herself, the light and the dark, bouncing back and forth between the two in order to find the middle ground of clear vision. Because of this, the shaman, even after his formal training has ended, must continually revisit the well of shadow and light, returning to this stage of initiation in order to keep a check on power. It is only by knowing him or herself entirely that the shaman can distinguish between the pure, limitless heart voice and the one that is filtered and distorted through the disowned parts of the self.

Revelation

The Purification/Purgation phase of the initiation is, for all these reasons, a torturous one for the initiate to endure. And yet, throughout this period of suffering, flashes of illumination and revelation into the cosmic consciousness that the initiate so desperately seeks break through the darkness and keep him or her moving forward toward the light at the end of the very dark tunnel. Through these challenges of both physical and emotional deprivation, the initiate begins to experience a shift in consciousness as the darker and ego-binding elements of his or her character are purged away. Once again, the initiate emerges into a state much like that of the Calling/Awakening phase, walking along the very thin boundary between life and death, self and selflessness. As each layer peels away and the individual's consciousness expands further outward to meet it, the initiate revels in a loving and joyous relationship to the Absolute and a new lightness of being. As he or she moves from darkness to lightness, from ego to unity, the initiate finds him or herself in that middle place of the mesa, the thin boundary between the limited self and the infinite. In this place of heightened awareness and consciousness, the shaman-in-training can look at the leaf of a tree and see a reflection of the cosmos. In this illuminated state, the boundaries have blurred to an extent where the shaman can perceive the interconnectedness of every living thing, which exists as a living expression of the Divine.

It is at this time that the initiate typically begins formal training in techniques of ecstasy that allow the shaman to consciously engage with his or her experiences in non-ordinary reality. Besides learning to master trance states, the shaman-in-training must also learn other "tricks of the trade" that connect ordinary reality to non-ordinary reality, such as conducting specific rituals and healing techniques, divining signs and omens in nature, and all other forms of expanding his or her perception within ordinary reality. Often this training process will go on for years, until the elders or spirit guides decide that the time has come for the shaman to reenter the world to share the knowledge and power that he or she has been given.

Worldly Return

"Worldly Return" is the phase of the spiritual journey that distinguishes the shaman from many of the other spiritual traditions throughout the world. Whereas the goal of certain mystical traditions may be to remain permanently in this unitive state to, as the mystics suggest, dissolve like a salt doll into the sea of God, the shaman returns from his mysterious adventure ready to share his newly bestowed gifts of knowledge with his community. In some cultures, the new shaman will perform a symbolic gesture to show his community what he has learned, such as climbing a tree or some other indication that he is now able to climb the center pillar and travel between the three worlds. From that moment on, the shaman becomes the spiritual liaison of his community, acting in numerous roles as priest, healer, counselor, and ceremonial leader. Having gone through death and returned, the shaman can comfortably and safely go back and forth between these realms, escort souls to or from the other worlds, and bring back information for the good of his or her community.

Spiritual Renewal

This cycle of initiatory death and rebirth, pleasure and pain, never really ends for the shaman. Once the calling is accepted, he or she takes on a lifetime of initiations, even after the formal apprenticeship has ended. He or she must continually undergo this process of transformation in order to grow and face each new challenge that is presented to him or her as a healer.

For a period of time after the Worldly Return there is often a sense of spiritual self-satisfaction on behalf of the shaman.

Inevitably, however, at some point during his or her practice, the shaman will come to a place where the transformation of consciousness gained during the initial calling and training is no longer enough. The shaman will invariably be faced with the understanding that, instead of the complete transcendence that was hoped for, he or she has only replaced the old set of preconceived with a new—albeit wider—set of blinders. This revelation, and the despair and frustration that invariably follows it, is what is called by mystical traditions a "dark night of the soul." With the rug pulled out from under him or her once again, the shaman finds him or herself back in the role of initiate, floating once again in the abyss of the purification stage. If the shaman is committed to moving even further down the path toward divine union, the initiation cycle will begin again—and again, and again, and again, continually enlarging the boundaries of spiritual consciousness and allowing for the shaman's greater depth of movement towards total mergence with Spirit.

In the words of Joseph Campbell, author of *The Power of Myth*:

> We have only to follow the thread of the hero's path, and where we had thought to find an abomination, we shall find a god. And where we had thought to slay another, we shall slay ourselves. Where we had thought to travel outward, we will come to the center of our own existence. And where we had thought to be alone, we will be with all the world.[17]

Exercises

Exercise #6: Recognizing Your Own Initiatory Ordeal

Life is constantly initiating us, if only we are paying attention. This is true for all of us, whether we are actively on a spiritual path or not. Birth, death, divorce, puberty, marriage, illness—these things are as much forms of initiation into a new stage of life as any spiritual calling. But are you using your ordeal for greater growth or merely trying to get through it? Unfortunately, those of us in modern society are often not trained to recognize our own life trials as achievements and teachings. Perhaps if we had the mindset or context to respect these ordeals as such, we could look at such difficulties as opportunities for growth and power instead of deepening evidence of the unfairness of life. This exercise is geared toward reframing your attitude to the events, both the joyful and the difficult, that have marked your life.

Prepare your space and yourself. Breathe. In your notebook, write down the most significant moments in your life, starting with your earliest memory. Write down all your recollections of each event. What people, living or in memory, guided you through each process? Who or what helped and guided you through that time? What obstacles did you encounter? What did you learn about yourself and about life? Was there a moment when you became courageous in your own eyes or lost courage? What strengths did you discover in yourself? What weaknesses? How has that event shaped the person that you are today? What powers have you acquired that can be used to reach a goal or a dream that you have? Always give thanks for these experiences, as they are your greatest teachers.

Design a ritual for yourself to honor these moments as significant initiatory experiences. I suggest that you pick one experience at first, the one you feel has been most influential to your growth, and focus the ritual on that. (For ideas on how to structure a ritual, refer to Chapter 5.) Create an altar to honor and give thanks to those guides that have assisted you in your path and ask for their continued support. If you feel comfortable, invite others to join your ritual and act as witnesses.

Exercise #7: Beginning the Process of Self-Discovery

As we have seen throughout this chapter, one of the main functions of the shaman's spiritual crisis and subsequent initiatory practices is the unveiling of the self. This includes uncovering the dark and light aspects of the self, which must be understood and embraced as part of the shaman's basis of power. This process can be difficult, and one may find him or herself wrestling with trying to discover what authentic parts of the self exist underneath the social conditioning of right and wrong, acceptable and unacceptable. This exercise is to help you uncover who you authentically are beneath all that training. What are your strengths and weaknesses? Your fears and doubts? What are you most proud of? This is an opportunity to go deep into yourself.

I am a big fan of psychotherapy as a tool for self-exploration, because it allows the opportunity to have an objective person—the psychotherapist—reflect your own patterns that you may not be consciously aware of. Outside of that, the best exercise I have found for getting in touch with one's inner self is free-flow writing (and I suppose one could modify this exercise to include "free-flow dance" or "free-flow painting"). In this exercise I want to encourage that you find a close friend with whom you can share things that came up for you during this exercise to act as a support system.

First, prepare yourself and your space. Sit down with your journal and a pen that is easy to write with. Begin to write whatever comes to your mind. You can present yourself with a topic if you like, such as, "What or who am I most afraid of?"; "What are my gifts?"; "What or who most angers me/fills me with strength?"; or "Who do I give my power away to?" Alternatively, simply write whatever is foremost in your mind at the time. See what is circling just under the surface of your conscious awareness, waiting to be uncovered. Keep your pen moving. Don't stop to think or to edit. Don't be afraid of tangents or non sequiturs. If you draw a blank, just write gibberish over and over until something comes spilling out of you. When it gets hard, that is the time to keep going. Continue as long as you can, but for at least 15 minutes. When you are done, ground yourself immediately and walk away. We will come back to this work in a later exercise.

Continuing this exercise on a regular basis can help you to uncover more and more things about yourself and help you recognize your own inner truth. Although we may find out things about ourselves that make us uncomfortable or even upset, know that these parts of yourself are, when recognized and used constructively, the greatest assets to your own power. Jungian analyst Robert A. Johnson maintains that the greatest "gold" in ourselves—that which is most brilliant, powerful, and needed in the world—comes from this shadow place within ourselves. It may be hard to imagine, but that area of ourselves and our lives that we have the hardest time with is often our greatest strength and power masquerading under layers of fear. As fear is the antithesis of love, and love the gateway to a deep connection to the cosmos, once this fear has been exorcised out of the shadows, our greatest strength and power can flow freely.

Chapter 3

The Shaman's Doorway: Journeys Into Ecstasy

T he word *ecstasy* comes from the Greek word *ekstasis*, which literally means "standing outside of or transcending oneself."[1] Shamanic ecstasy is defined by a process in which, through any one of a number of intentional means, the shaman separates his or her soul from the body, releasing it to travel into one or more of the three spirit worlds.[2] During the Calling phase of the initiation, the neophyte shaman had little to no control over his or her experience within these states. Throughout the apprenticeship, then, the initiate must begin the rigorous practices of going back and forth into these states at will. Within these mythical, archetypal realms of spirit, the candidate learns how to navigate his or her way around the cosmos, becoming familiar with the topography of non-ordinary reality. Through the discipline of continual practice within these states, the neophyte learns how to turn crude, nonsensical journeys into lucid visions in which he or she is the participant, observer, and controller. It is here in these realms that the shaman-in-training meets and begins to establish or reestablish relationships with spirit allies, many of whom may have come to the candidate during the near-death or abduction experience of the Awakening/Calling phase. This is a vital stage of learning for the apprentice, for these relationships with personal helping spirits are the basis of the shaman's power. Shamans cannot function without the help of spirit allies who instruct and protect the shaman throughout his or her journeys.

Shamanism is by no means the only spiritual tradition whose practitioners employ the use of transformative ecstatic states. The achievement of ecstasy is the primary goal of many forms of religious experience, in particular the mystical traditions of the world. Both the shaman and the mystic are uniquely adept at being able to enter into a trance state and move their consciousness to worlds beyond that of normal experience. Both involve similar means of generating these states, and both experience ecstasies that follow a similar pattern, starting with the process of purification and purgation of the self, followed by revelation and divine union. Because of these similarities, as well as other parallels in language and content, it is easy for the outside observer to confuse the two as being the same. However, the intent behind the process is where the mystic and the shaman part ways. For the mystic, complete mergence with the sacred is the goal of the practitioner's spiritual ascent and, therefore, its final end. Shamanism, on the other hand, is a system in which the primary goal is a "magical" transformation of the physical world. Unlike that of the mystic, the shaman's ecstasy continues on past the Revelation stage, culminating with the Worldly Return in which the shaman rejoins the realm of the physical in order to use the information gained within these altered states.

Evelyn Underhill points out the difference between the mystic and the magician in her 1911 book, *Mysticism*:

Both claim that they give their initiates powers unknown to ordinary men. But...the ends to which those
powers are applied differ enormously. In mysticism
the will is united with the emotions in an impassioned
desire to transcend the sense-world, in order that the
self may be joined by love to the one eternal and ultimate Object of love; whose existence is intuitively perceived by that which we used to call the soul.... In
magic, the will unites with the intellect in an impassioned desire for supersensible knowledge.[3]

These two distinct and fundamental goals create a significant contrast between two very similar spiritual experiences.
Many mystical traditions—often existing side by side with
shamanism, as in the case of Tibetan Buddhism and the Bon
shamanic tradition—tend to be leery of the shaman's "magical" and "manipulative" practices and the potential that exists
for them to be used for negative means.

Besides those of the mystic, the shaman's trance states
are also distinguished from other ecstatics that involve direct
communication with the spirit world, such as mediums and
other spiritualists. In these cases, there is a similar transmission of information using the spiritual practitioner as com-
municant. However, these other experiences involve a
sometimes-involuntary possession by the spirits in which the
person receiving the transmission is disassociated from his or
her self and therefore has no conscious awareness of or control
over this transmission of knowledge. In contrast, the experience of the shaman is a cooperative effort with his or her spirit
allies. During the time of the ecstasy, the shaman remains in
total control of the experience, entering and exiting at will and
being able to recall and utilize the information gathered during
these sessions for the good of the individual or community. Re-
taining some form of awareness throughout the experience is
vital, as the focus is always on the shaman's ability to bring back
information that can be recalled and implemented in a way

that can be put into action for the good of the people. Even those shamanic traditions that refer to the shaman's ecstasies as a "possession" rather than a "soul journey," such as in the Korean or Tibetan traditions, maintain that the shaman remains aware and in control of his or her experiences during the process.

A similar set of principles apply when attempting to delineate the differences between the Shamanic State of Consciousness (SSC)[4] and other, non-intentional forms of altered states of consciousness, such as chaotic drug states, dreaming (except in cases of lucid dreaming), daydreaming, near-death experiences, and other forms of uncontrolled flight. Simply put, although all SSCs involve going into altered states, not all forms of altered states can be considered SSCs. This is not to downplay the importance of these other states, by any means. As we have seen, the near-death experience is often the precursor to subsequent journeys into the SSC, and dreams have long been regarded as containing messages from the spirit realm. However, according to the strictest definition of the SSC, which I will apply here, these states lack the two vital elements that distinguish the shaman's particular brand of ecstasy: a specified intention and a combination of both conscious and unconscious control over the ecstatic experience.

In order to satisfy these two conditions, the shaman must, once again, become a master of balance. Unlike the mystical traditions in which the goal is the total dissolution of the self, what makes the shaman's journeys so unique and useful is that the shaman is able to remain conscious and connected while, at the same time, fluid enough to allow for the voice of spirit to come through. In this way, the shaman is able to maintain a foothold in each world, a simultaneous awareness of both ordinary and non-ordinary reality. These other forms of altered awareness, on the other hand, usually involve the individual falling too far to one side or the other to retrieve information successfully. For example, although dream- and drug-induced euphoria can often resemble shamanic states of consciousness in form and content, they cannot be considered "ecstatic" experiences because the conscious mind is too far removed from the experience to allow for either controlled and intentional exploration or accurate recall of the information gathered. In the case of daydreams, the exact opposite is true. In this case, the mind becomes a kind of closed circuit, receiving images only from the conscious mind and allowing for very little input from the unconscious or spirit mind.

Here again we arrive at a sacred paradox of trying to make two seemingly opposite tasks occur at once and come together in perfect balance. As with dark and light, ego mind and spirit mind, during these ecstatic flights the shaman must walk that tenuous razor-thin line of both controlling and releasing the conscious mind, engaging in a dance of being solid and flowing, wave particle and matter, all at once. Many of us are familiar with that hazy space that we fall into in those brief moments between wakefulness and sleep. In those in-between spaces, the mind is still conscious of its own thoughts and, yet, those thoughts often seem to originate from someplace outside of the self. This is a hard zone to hold. Too often we find ourselves falling to one side or the other, losing footing in this state by either reemerging into full consciousness or sliding down into the depths of sleep. It is in learning to walk this fine line that the shaman earns the title "Master of Ecstasy."

The second most important factor in the shaman's journey is intent. Without purpose, the shaman and his experiences would be of little to no help to his community, for having vision is not the same as having the ability to apply that vision concretely in the physical world. In his role as mediator between flesh and spirit, the shaman might choose to enter nonordinary reality for any number of reasons pertaining to the community or individual's needs. Most typically these include:

1. To act as a *psychopomp*, or "leader of souls," the shaman enters non-ordinary reality in order to escort the souls of the deceased into the next world or, conversely, to retrieve a lost or stolen soul and return it to an individual.

2. As healer or diagnostician of the community, the shaman makes this journey in order to both diagnose the patient's affliction and to ask for help from spirit guides on the best way to treat the individual. This also refers to any kind of healing on a larger level than just the individual, such as afflictions affecting the community or planet.

3. As *soothsayer*, the shaman steps outside of linear time in order to divine information about past, present, or future events.

In these states of ecstasy, time, place, and physical limitations cease to exist, allowing the shaman to access any form of information that is needed but that may not be accessible via "typical" means. In Chapter 1, I stated that "through self-induced states of ecstasy—trances—the shaman's mind becomes a radio to attune to the frequencies of the universe. In these states a kind of 'sympathetic resonance' occurs. The shaman's soul, now released from the confines of the physical, ascends or descends into one or more of these worlds by way of the axis mundi, the center axis of the world." As we saw in the last chapter, the shaman's first experience entering into a state of ecstasy is often during the Calling/Awakening phase of his or her initiation. This change in vibrational resonance is often provoked by a physical or mental illness that transforms the shaman's consciousness to the point where he or she achieves that sympathetic resonance and is thereby propelled unwittingly into the spirit world. After that first unintentional encounter, the neophyte shaman must find ways of entering into these states purposefully and consciously.

Techniques of Ecstasy

Shamans across the world, from both indigenous and modern cultures, have all found a variety of means by which to enter into this sympathetic resonance, various vehicles to help open the channels of communication to the spirit world and facilitate the visionary experience. These include, but are not limited to, the ritual use of hallucinogenic drugs and plants, specialized movements and dance, chanting, rattling, and drumming, as well as visualization techniques that have recently gained popularity among westerners and is taught under the name of "Shamanic Journeying."

Plants of the Gods

The Tukano people of the Vaupes region of Columbia say that the first people came from the sky in a serpent canoe, and Father Sun promised them a magical drink that would connect them with the radiant powers of the heavens. While the men were in the "House of the Waters" attempting to make this drink, the first woman went into the forest to give birth. She came back with a boy radiating golden light, whose body she rubbed with leaves. This luminous boy child was the vine, and each of the men cut off a piece of this living being, which became his piece of the vine lineage.[5]

The origin of the shamanic use of psychotropic plants dates back thousands of years. In fact, the origin myths of many native people associate these sacred substances with the beginning of language, culture, and even the creation of humankind itself.[6] At the dawn of time, it is believed, the gods gave humankind these plants as a means of communicating with the heavens. Indigenous people, therefore, have a deep respect and reverence for these plant teachers, regarding them as embodiments of conscious intelligent beings who function as spiritual guides and sources of healing power and knowledge.[7]

Anthropological and ethnobotanical investigations have made certain rites involving these plant spirit medicines well known to the western world, such as the peyote pilgrimages of the Huichol Indians of Mexico, the use of iboga by the African Bwiti tradition, and the ayahuasca ceremonies of the South America *vegalistas*.[8] In these cultures, the insights gleaned through ingesting these consciousness-expanding plants are considered important medicines for the healing of the individual and the community. In *The Way of the Shaman*, Michael Harner noted that an interesting distinction between shamanic healing practices and western medicine is that in order for the healing to take place, it is often the shaman, not the patient, who takes the plant medicine.[9]

Earlier in the chapter, I mentioned that "chaotic drug states" were *not* considered true SSCs. This is true, although the stress in this statement should be on the word *chaotic*, which is to imply a hallucinogenic state that is entered into without intent and with such a high dosage as to render the journey nonsensical and impractical. Unlike the indiscriminate use of mind-altering drugs that now plagues western society, shamanic practices involve careful dosages and preparations, which physically, mentally, and spiritually prepare the shaman for his or her journey. Before embarking on a practice, the shaman has usually undergone extensive training with the plant medicine (including developing a deep and mutually honoring relationship with the spirit of that plant), in order to ensure that he or she will not get lost within the vision and will be able to maintain control and focus throughout the length of the journey.

Pharmacological studies have pinpointed various phytochemicals within each of the plants that change the chemistry of the mind in such a way as to produce these visionary experiences. But, although science can explain the chemical alchemy that takes place in the human brain during these states, it does not have an explanation for the contents of the experiences themselves, nor does it explain the fact that the contents of the visions vary very little from individual to individual, culture to culture, indicating that these experiences transcend culturally based belief systems. Researchers studying the effects of LSD on westerners in the 1950s found that the subjects would slip into states remarkably similar to those experienced by the shaman during his or her flights into ecstasy.[10]

In *The Holographic Universe*, Michael Talbot recounts the findings of researcher Stanislov Grof, who experimented with the clinical uses of LSD. During these experiments, the subjects slipped into a state of consciousness much like those of the shamans during their ecstasies in which they felt a sense of oneness with the cosmos. Talbot writes:

> They seemed capable of knowing what it was like to be every animal, and even plant, on the tree of evolution. They could experience what it was like to be a blood cell, an atom, thermonuclear process inside the sun, the consciousness of the entire planet, and even the consciousness of entire cosmos. More than that, they displayed the ability to transcend space and time, and occasionally they related uncannily accurate precognitive information. In an even stranger vein they sometimes encountered non-human intelligences during their cerebral travels, discarnate beings, spirit guides from "higher planes of consciousness," and other superhuman entities. On occasion subjects also traveled to what appeared to be other universe and other levels of reality.[11]

In many indigenous societies, these "plants of the gods" play an indispensable role in the practices of the healing shamans. However, there are those who argue that plant- or drug-induced states cannot be considered "true ecstatic methods."[12] Mircea Eliade considered them lesser means of reaching an ecstatic state, saying that, "in shamanism itself, narcotics already represent a decadence" and that "in default of true ecstatic methods, recourse is taken to narcotics to induce trance."[13] Even Carlos Castaneda, whose books describing his frequent use of peyote during his apprenticeship with the Toltec *nagual*[14] Don Juan Matus made him a kind of patron saint to the psychedelic revolution, later discouraged the use of psychoactive substances as a means to ecstasy. In an interview with Sam Keen in 1972, Castaneda said, "Don Juan used psychotropic plants only in the middle period of my apprenticeship because I was so stupid, sophisticated and cocky. I held on to my description of the world as if it were the only truth. Psychotropics created a gap in my system of glosses.[15] They destroyed my dogmatic certainty. But I paid a tremendous price. When the glue that held my world together was dissolved, my body was weakened and it took months to recuperate. I was anxious and functioned at a very low level."[16]

The Rhythm Method

Ayahuasca and other such spirit plant medicines, when used with the utmost care and in the proper context, can be valuable tools for helping an individual understand the landscape of an SSC. When done intentionally and in a spiritual context, these spirit allies can act as keys to open doors in the consciousness that are very often kept firmly shut by the ego mind. However, in my opinion, for the majority of people, these "training wheels" must come off eventually in order to have true freedom within this state. In western society, in particular, regular use of such substances is impractical, not to mention illegal. The visionary must therefore work to keep these doors of consciousness open without relying on outside stimuli that may, in the end, hinder his or her progress. Besides, although the use of psychotropic drugs and plants may represent a significant tool in the shaman's initial movement into ecstasy, they are only one of many highly developed techniques. Studies in neurochemistry have shown that the brain carries its own consciousness-altering drugs that can be stimulated through other means.

For example, some form of repetitive movement or dance is often employed by the shaman during ritual in order to thrust him or herself into a state of ecstasy. Holgar Kalweit noted that these monotonous movements were a prerequisite for higher states of consciousness, causing the psyche to withdraw from its ordinary engagement with the external world and move into deeper levels of consciousness. In ordinary reality—and especially so in the modern world—the amount of external stimuli is so great that it becomes more and more challenging to quiet the mind. Once the stream of stimuli is reduced, the psyche begins to produce its own experiences, opening itself up to new dimensions of experience.[17]

Tribal shamans may dance for hours during ceremony, working themselves past the limits of endurance, into a frenzied state in which their minds suddenly disconnect from their physical bodies, leaving their souls free to travel the cosmos unimpeded. These movements often involve mimicking the sounds and movements of certain animals. This is due to the belief that animal spirits move easily between the worlds. By embodying the energetic patterns of a particular animal, taking on its essence, the shaman is able to travel with a similar ease.

Very often shamanic rituals involve using sound, often some sort of repetitive noise, such as rhythmic chanting or the sounding of percussive instruments (rattling and drumming, for example), as a vehicle for the ecstatic state. Although it is fairly easy for us to understand how sacred plants cause such an impressive transformation of consciousness, what is more compelling is the profound effect that these non-chemical stimuli have on the individual. It is with good reason that Siberian and other shamans refer to the drum as the vehicle, sometimes referred to as the "horse" or "canoe," that transports them into the various realms. Modern scientific research into the effects of rhythmic sound have discovered that the electrical rhythms of the brain tend to assume the same rhythm as that of its stimulus, creating, yet again, a sympathetic resonance. Maintained for a period of at least 13 to 15 minutes, rhythmic drumming, rattling, and chanting have been proven to stimulate right brain activity, thereby inducing altered states of consciousness that contain imagery just as vivid as the ones experienced by those ingesting psychotropic plants.

To understand this concept involves a bit of explanation of the inner workings of the human brain. Within the brain, four major types of brainwave patterns or frequency bands have been isolated, each emitting a different number of cycles per second. They are called (in order of fastest to slowest) beta, alpha, theta, and delta. When a person is engaging in daily life, walking, talking, paying the bills, and so on, the brain operates in beta, a high-frequency range of 12 to 18 hertz (cycles per second). The brain pulses in beta during times of anxiety and fear, suggesting that one of the functions of this frequency is to focus on physical survival. The alpha state, measuring from eight to 12 hertz, is considered the brain's "neutral" and is associated with states of relaxation in which consciousness is altered and internalized. Theta waves, forming a pattern of four to eight hertz, are most evident in the state in between waking and sleep and are distinguished by a near-unconscious state that often inundates the individual with intense and often unexpected imagery. Theta is considered by many to be the place of deep and deliberate meditation. Delta, which occurs when the brainwave frequency goes below four hertz, is the longest and slowest wave, is associated with deep sleep or unconsciousness.[18]

In the 1960s, researcher Andrew Neher investigated the effects of drumming on EEG patterns in the human brain. He found that rhythmic drumming produces changes in the central nervous system, affecting the electrical activity in many of the sensory and motor areas of the brain. A pattern that incorporated approximately four to four and a half beats per second, what Neher called "auditory driving," was found to be the most efficient for inducing theta states. Neher concluded that certain sound waves, such as those produced by percussion instruments, have specific neuro-physical effects that can elicit temporary changes in the brainwave activity of an individual. Furthermore, he discovered that pulses that matched alpha brain waves at between eight and 13 hertz lead to similar sensory and imagery bombardment as with the SSC.[19] In *A Symphony in the Brain*, Jim Robbins wrote: "Reports from alpha-theta clients frequently go far to the edge of strangeness, and spiritual experiences—encounters with Jesus or dead relatives or other spirits are not uncommon."[20]

Shamanic Journeying

Shamans, whether they relate to it in such scientific terms or not, instinctively understand the implications of brainwaves on reality and use this understanding for transporting themselves to other vibratory states of consciousness. With dedicated practice, what can be accomplished with external stimuli, it seems, can also be re-created in the brain by force of will alone. Research into brainwave biofeedback[21] in the late 1950s showed that individuals can be taught how to change their brain's electrical signals and produce certain frequencies at will.[22] In 1978, brainwave researcher Elmer Green traveled to India in order to study eastern holy men using various scientific tools and methods. Green found that these yogis had the ability to move quickly between brainwave frequencies, moving almost instantly from beta, waking consciousness, to a deep meditative alpha state.[23]

This technique of consciously altering brainwave activity through deep meditative and hypnotic states is one of the main ecstatic methods of the shaman, and especially those emerging from non-shamanic societies. Westerners were introduced to this technique (still taught under the name of "Shamanic

Journeying") in 1980, with the publication of Michael Harner's classic book on cross-cultural shamanism, *The Way of the Shaman*. Using a variety of relaxation techniques and rhythmic drumming, the individual embarking upon a shamanic journey enters into a deep meditative state in which his or her brainwaves slow from the rapid wave of beta, which, in a usual state of affairs, overwhelms consciousness, to the slower undulations of alpha-theta waves. He or she then visualizes him or herself as diving down through a hole in the earth into the Lower World or, conversely, making an ascent to the Upper World realms. From here the individual's mind is let loose to wander the cosmos, allowing a flood of images to spontaneously emerge. Very often the individual enters into the journey seeking guidance with a question or concern. Typically, much of the journey, therefore, involves seeking out spirit allies to help him or her gain the necessary insight and information. Unlike ecstatic conditions induced by psychotropics or other outer stimuli, shamanic journeying allows the practitioner to enter in and out of these states anywhere and for whatever length of time is needed or is convenient. This is a very user-friendly technique for the practitioner, who can then quickly access information from the spirit world wherever and whenever needed. I have heard of practitioners who go into these states while riding the subway or in the middle of business meetings. The shamanic journey process makes it possible to have quick and efficient access to the spirit world through the doorway of the unconscious, allowing the individual to engage in useful dialogues with the inhabitants of these realms.

Travels Into Ecstasy

By whatever means he or she attains this state, once the shaman finds the gateway to transforming his or her consciousness, he or she is able to step out of ordinary reality and into the axis mundi, the transition point between the worlds. To the mind's eye, this middle place is often represented in visions as some form of symbolic "crossing over place," such as the world tree, a bridge, a ladder, or a rainbow. One could speculate that generating these symbols is the mind's way of expressing a crossing over from one thing to another, from conscious to unconscious, from physical to spirit. In biological terms, it may symbolically represent the journey of the mind's consciousness across the *corpus collosum*, the middle area that separates left and right brain, logical and intuitive thinking. This is the void, the place "betwixt and between," what in the Jewish shamanic tradition is called the realm of "Beyond the Pargod," the thin veil that separates spirit from matter.[24] It is here that the two levels of reality, the spirit and the physical, merge, flowing into one another like two rivers joining to form one powerful stream.

In this middle place, the shaman's soul is free to travel into the other realms, into the Middle, Lower, and/or Upper Worlds. In these states, the individual is bombarded by a flow of images or sensations[25] that bubble up out of the unconscious and provide the shaman with needed information. Each journey is an adventure, a passage into a limitless place of dreamlike images in which the rules of time and space as we know them in the physical world are suspended. Here the shaman comes in contact with his or her spirit allies who assist the shaman in his or her journey. These allies can present themselves in many forms, from the images of gods and goddesses of various traditions, to the souls of dead ancestors (especially ancestral shamans), to power animals or plant or mineral guides.

Imagination

Rationalists often pass off the shaman's experiences during ecstasy as aimless wanderings of the imagination. Unfortunately, in western culture we have been brought up to view the imagination as some meaningless psychological function involving a mental projection of something not real or present. Indigenous people, on the other hand, take for granted the reality of these inner worlds. For them, imagination is simply another mode of perception, a doorway through which the human and divine worlds can interact. One of the greatest difficulties for those of us coming from a western-based mindset is learning to transcend this collective prejudice that distinguishes the "real" from the "unreal." In the shamanic way of thinking, these states are not a deviation from reality, but they allow us to access an aspect of it that remains hidden in an ordinary state of consciousness.

Says Malidoma Somé, a shaman of the Dagara tradition of West Africa:

> Western culture has made a distinction between what is real and what is not real, while in my culture, there isn't any subdivision. Your dreams are just as real as any concrete thing you can touch, smell, and sense. Your intuition, your imagination—all of these things are a part of a reality that is as concrete as anything else is. Anything the human imagination has access to is just as real as anything else. The modern world is going to have to get to that place sooner or later, one way or another. Because it *is* real.[26]

In his book, *Man, God, and Magic*, ethnologist Ivar Lissner wrote: "I believe that the only truths are imagination, the soul, and inspiration."[27]

Metaphor and Symbol: The Language of Spirit

The best way for the western mind to get past this collective prejudice that imagination isn't "real" is by continually practicing this process. Once the images and dialogues within these states are proven to provide accurate and useful information, it is no longer so easy to pass off the information as unsubstantiated "imagination" or "fantasy." When I became aware of this after seeing the remarkable results of my own journeys, everything in my life changed for me. Suddenly,

I found myself connected to a whole new place from which to source information about my relationships, my work— everything. Viewing my own mind as a vehicle for the voice of spirit opened up a whole new dimension of possibility and potential for my life that I had once discounted.

Part of the process of becoming adept at receiving this information is learning to interpret divine messages in the language in which the spirit world best expresses itself through the human mind. As in a dream, journeys to the other planes of existence take the individual to a place where language and logic are replaced by a communication system made up largely of symbols. The language of spirit is one of poetry, of metaphor, and because of this the visionary experience of the neophyte shaman may seem nonsensical at first. The talent of the shaman is that, through continual practice, he or she eventually transcends the symbols as codes and is able to perceive these spiritual realities directly.

To illustrate this idea, I'll give an example from my own experience. One morning, I woke up with a deep, burning pain in my stomach. The pain lasted for several days without relief. I took myself into a journey with the question, "What is the cause of my pain?" Once in a deep meditative state, I found myself walking through a garden filled with leafy green plants. The plants spread out around me in every direction, as far as my eyes could see, and had an overwhelmingly pungent smell that was so strong that I found myself almost nauseated by it. Although the smell was familiar, I couldn't place it. Before I had taken my first step, I heard a thump in front of me. A large, pulpy tomato rolled out from under the plants and settled at my feet. It was then that I recognized the smell as that of the tomato plant. Suddenly, there were more thumps, and then more and more. Dozens of tomatoes came rolling at me, filling the space from all directions. Though I was somewhat amused by this surrealistic vision of this strange tomato world, I was frustrated that the journey was not succeeding in giving me an answer to my question. I tried to will the tomatoes away, but they kept coming, more and more, until they filled the space completely. I ended the journey feeling that I hadn't accomplished much at all. I certainly didn't have an answer to my question.

The next day, my doctor easily diagnosed the pain as the beginnings of an ulcer, most likely caused by stress and eating too many spicy and acidic foods. I took this news in stride and didn't try to make any connections between it and the images I had seen in my journey. Later that same afternoon, I spoke with a close friend of mine and told him about the diagnosis. He was sympathetic. As it turned out, he had had a similar problem a few summers earlier. That year he had decided to plant a vegetable garden in his backyard. Although most of the vegetables he had seeded in had not been successful, the tomato plants grew out of control until they took over the entire garden. Soon, he had more tomatoes than he knew what to do with. Not wanting to waste them, he spent the entire summer eating tomato sandwiches, tomato soup, spaghetti sauce—any tomato concoction he could think of—for every meal. After a few months of this diet, his stomach began to burn ferociously until he was diagnosed—sure enough—as having the beginnings of an ulcer. When he told his doctor about his recent diet, the doctor pinpointed the tomatoes, with their high acid content, as being the cause.

Had I continued to journey on that question—perhaps if I had tried restating that question in a simpler way, for instance—I might very well have been shown the answer to my question in a way that I would understand and saved myself a trip to the doctor. At the time, however, I was stubborn and impatient and lacked confidence in my own process. As it is with learning any language, in time and with practice, such dialogues between the conscious and unconscious mind can eventually become easily understood. As there is no Rosetta Stone of the spirit world, in order to become fluent in this metaphorical language, the journeyer must become familiar with his or her own personalized symbol system.

Symbols reach us at different levels. Some are universal, part of what Jung called the "collective unconscious," a well of knowledge and memory located within the inherited structure of the mind and, therefore, a part of all common human experience. According to Jung, the collective unconscious contains a collection of archetypes, universal images and ideas that are common to the experience of every human being. The ancients knew the power of this experience and turned these shamanic journeys into stories that later became known to us as myths. Despite the passing of time, these myths remain with us today, captivating us with their rich, primordial symbology, and reminding us at some level that such battles between light and dark are fought every day within the cosmos and ourselves.

Other symbols reach us at a societal level, at what might be called the "cultural unconscious," born out of the myths of a particular society. Although the "collective unconscious" may explain why most shamanic practices around the world follow similar patterns, the "cultural unconscious" is responsible for the specific trappings within which these practices take place. For example, in the practices of the Huichol shamans of Mexico, the deer is the animal spirit that is traditionally associated with acting as intermediary between the physical and spirit worlds. When asked why the deer in particular was chosen as the totem animal, Huichol elder don José Matsuwa responded, "Well, do you see any elephants around here?"[28]

Most important and, ironically, often the most challenging are the symbols that come to the shaman on a personal level and are understandable only to the shaman him or herself. These messages are custom-made by the universe for the shaman's personal use, drawn off of his or her own individual system of symbols, and cannot be deciphered or decoded by anyone else. For example, during a journey, two shamans may each individually receive the image of a snake slithering across their path. For one, the snake may convey danger, indicating the need to turn back from their present course of action. For another, this same snake could mean that a significant transformation lies up ahead or that the shaman (or client) must shed his or her skin before continuing on.

Despite the often-arbitrary nature of the images, given the chance, most images inevitably come clear if worked with long enough. This is another reason why it is so important for anyone embarking upon these journeys to "know thyself," to do an inner exploration of the self in order to understand the symbolic paradigms that relates to them on a personal level. It is also why it is so important to go into a journey with a specific question that needs to be addressed. The more specific the question, the more clearly the answer will come. Fortunately, for those of us who learn slowly, the spirits will often continue to put this same message in front of us in as many ways is needed until we understand. Over time and with practice, this metaphorical language becomes second nature, allowing one access to a hidden world of unlimited information.

The Shaman's Ecstasies

These journeys into ecstasy are the hallmark of the shaman and are what makes him or her so useful to the people of his or her community. These techniques are at once both simple and excruciatingly difficult, for, although entrance into these ecstatic states takes only trust and faith, establishing enough trust and faith to allow the process to unfold is one of the most challenging undertakings that the shaman encounters on his or her path. Each ecstatic journey involves a reenactment of the initiation process, in which the shaman must travel past the boundaries separating life from death, transcend all duality, and re-emerge within an intangible realm. Here the shaman is confronted with demi-gods and demons, forces of the universe and aspects of ourselves that wish to both create and destroy.

The shaman must therefore have confidence not only in his or her own ability to navigate safely through this ocean of vibration but also, as Oscar Miro-Quesada says:

> [trust] that God, the *Pacha*, the universal world, is a safe place to float. It's knowing that even if you become tired of floating or trying to swim with the current, you'll never drown. Your dedication to being of service to others is a guarantee that you will arrive at your destination without needing to know exactly how you got there. So it is embracing the great mystery and knowing that it is a user-friendly universe.... When you leave a place of safety, a familiar space, you are always going to be required to leave behind your personal will, the need to control, to be in charge. For a true shamanic journey, you need to be put aside. You need to let divine will to just take over and to trust that there is a larger being, a larger source that is guiding you and directing your journey.[29]

In the chapters that follow, we will further explore the shaman's experiences in ecstasy, the spirit allies that he or she meets there, and the function of SSCs as a vital element in the shaman's ritual and healing practices.

Exercises

Although there are a variety of ways for one to get into a Shamanic State of Consciousness, the safest and easiest way for most people, especially those who are doing the work on their own, to get into this state is through Shamanic Journeying. When preparing to journey, preparation of space and self takes a few extra steps and a few more accoutrements. The best (and most popular) way I have found to journey is through using the sound of the drum to help get you into these states. As we have discussed, the rhythm of the drum is conducive to creating brainwave patterns that help one slip into an SSC more easily.[30] Many people have had success using relaxing, non-verbal music as well.

Prepare yourself and your space, also being sure to prepare whatever music you have chosen so that it is audible but not too loud or distracting. You can, of course, journey in silence if you wish. Have a blanket near you in case you get cold. (Oftentimes undergoing any kind of meditation will cause the body temperature to drop, so be prepared.)

If you wish, you can memorize the steps to the following journeys so that you can do them alone. Or have a friend read them to you as you go until you are familiar enough with them to do it on your own. As you journey, get yourself into a similar mindset as when you do the free-flow writing exercise. Don't edit or change anything once it appears to you. Just keep going. Though some things may seem strange at first, don't discount any experience that you have here. In these worlds, all things are possible, limited only by the boundaries of your confidence in your own imagination. Remember that you are in a "free will zone." You can choose to leave or tell someone or something to go at any time.

Exercise #8: A Lower World Journey

Lay or sit down and close your eyes. Concentrate on breathing in through the nose and out through the mouth. Feel the flow of breath in and out of your lungs. Imagine yourself pulling in knowledge and power with each inhale. With each exhale, release any pain, discomfort, distraction, or worries that you may have. In this space and time they do not exist. Let them go.

Set your intent for this exercise. Formulate a question, such as, "Who are my allies in the Lower World?" or "What is my first step in overcoming ___ problem?" Your question is your intent and is the arrow that will carry you through the journey. As you become more experienced you will see that the question has an almost magical power. The formulation of it can be an insight in itself, for every question carries with it the seed of its own answer. When you are ready, ask for guidance and support from your allies during this journey.

Take a deep breath in and hold it, tightening all the muscles in your body, and then relaxing with one great exhale. Start with the muscles in your feet, ankles, calves, and shins. Hold the breath, tighten, and release. Then do the same with your thighs and buttocks. Hold the breath, tighten, and release. Repeat with your abdomen, chest, and back. Hold the breath, tighten, and release. Now the shoulders and forearms. Hold, tighten, and release. Now the head, neck, and face. Hold, tighten, and release. Now tighten the entire body at once. Hold, tighten, and release.

Imagine yourself within the Center Pillar. Pull the light down within you and feel its warmth as you become one with it. Picture yourself at the opening to a tunnel or some other opening into the earth that presents itself and is inviting to you. Enter into that opening, feeling yourself being pulled downward as if by a strong force. The opening drops you into the Lower World that you have designed for yourself. Look around at your surroundings. What else is there that you hadn't discovered before? Explore.

Now, find a place on the landscape that calls you to sit down. When you look up, you can see someone or something coming towards you. You are not afraid, because you know nothing can hurt you here. If you do get an unpleasant or uncomfortable feeling from the being's presence, ask it to leave and wait for another to appear. Watch (or sense) as the shape grows clearer and clearer. Perhaps instead of an image it "appears" as a strong feeling of some kind. What is it? A human? An animal? Something else? Even if it seems strange, go with it. The being sits down in front of you. Feel its welcoming presence. Get to know it. Perhaps you have a question that it can answer for you. Have a dialogue with this being.

When you are ready, or when you hear the call-back sound, finish up your conversation. Thank the being for coming and for any assistance that it may have given you. Stand up and go back to the entranceway that brought you here. Be sure to return the same way you came. This is important. Feel yourself being pulled upward through the opening you descended through, back into your body.

When you have done this, wiggle your toes and fingers to get you fully back into your body. Reconnect with your breath if need be. Ground yourself. When you are ready, open your eyes.

Record your experience in your journal.

Exercise #9: An Upper World Journey

Follow the same steps as in the previous exercise. This time, however, you will be going to the Upper World. After you are have gone through the preparation process, find an entrance to the Upper World via a ladder, an elevator, or some other means of ascent that is welcoming, is positive, and calls to you. At the end, remember to record your experience.

Exercise #10: A Middle World Journey

Again, you will be following the same steps as described in the Lower World journey exercise, with a few modifications. Instead of finding a means of descent into the ground or ascent into the sky, imagine yourself traveling horizontally across time and space. If you wish, find a location that you have physically been to before and have an experience there. Alternatively, find a place in the physical world that you would like to visit. Explore the landscape and continue dialoguing with whatever beings you find there. Come back the way you came. Record your experiences.

Chapter 4

Demi-Gods and Demons: The Shaman's Pantheon of Spirit Allies

"Therefore I judge it best that you should choose
To follow me, and I will be your guide
Away from here and through an eternal place"...
"From now, we two will share one will together:
You are my teacher, my master, my guide."
So I spoke, and when he moved I followed after
And entered on that deep and savage road."

—The Inferno

In Dante Alighieri's epic poem, *The Divine Comedy*, the reader follows Dante the narrator's journey through the three realms of death in order to overcome his earthly passions and discover his unity with God. When the tale begins, he is lost in a dark and foreboding forest. He sees a mountain above him, bathed in sunlight. He tries to ascend, but three menacing beasts block his way and force him to turn back. Frightened and helpless, he returns to the dark valley. There, he encounters the spirit of Virgil, the great Roman poet, who, Virgil tells him, has been sent to show him a different path up the mountain. Virgil offers his services as Dante's guide through "an eternal place." And so this partnership begins. Throughout the course of his journey, Virgil not only assists Dante in navigating the physical route, but he also repeatedly protects him from hostile demons and monsters and acts as mentor and counselor in times of need. At those times when Virgil's own limitations leave him unable to assist Dante, other spirits arrive to offer assistance.

This epic poem is a perfect allegory for the relationships that the shaman develops within his or her journeys through the invisible realms. Like Dante, the shaman is not dead, but a "living soul" who is able to traverse the worlds beyond death and return. In these journeys, the shaman comes in contact with the gods and demons of the non-ordinary realms, spirit beings concerned with human affairs and capable of helping or harming their interests. Although not all spirit beings that exist ally themselves to the shaman, during the beginning stages of the initiation the candidate is often "adopted" by one or more tutelary spirits. As with Dante's experience, it is usually during the time of greatest fear and loneliness during the initiation that the conscious mind quiets down, allowing the psychic self to open up enough to allow the spirit ally to reveal itself as guide and mentor.

Once revealed, the spirit then assists the shamanic candidate in the acquisition of power and knowledge. During the initiation, the neophyte often undergoes a spiritual dismemberment in which the tutelary spirit psychically tears the candidate into pieces and then reassembles him or her into a new form that imbues the shaman with some of the spirit's essence and power. Eliade calls the shaman's allies "mystical organs,"[1] for during this transformation, the candidate's essence becomes merged with that of the spirit helper, and, in some ways of thinking about it, the two become fused into one, establishing a kind of simultaneous existence together. In the Wiradjuri tribe of Australia, the tutelary spirit is called both *bala*, meaning "spirit companion," and *jarawaijewa*, meaning "the meat that is within him."[2] In some traditions it is believed that after this process of initiatory mergence, the souls of the spirit guardian and the shaman are so firmly linked that if the spirit ally chooses to leave, the shaman would die soon after.

Whether or not this is true to such an extreme extent is open to interpretation. However, all shamanic traditions agree that establishing and maintaining good relationships with spirit allies is of utmost importance to the shaman. As with anyone traveling to a new place, the shaman is dependent upon his or her spirit allies to help guide, protect, and assist in his or her quest for knowledge and empowerment.

Assistance from spirit allies is not exclusive to the shaman. All of us—whether we interact with them consciously or not—have spirit allies. But although it is believed that everyone in the physical world has spirit allies guiding them, the shaman is distinguished by his or her ability to engage in a back-and-forth dialogue with these entities, to ask for help, bargain with, and engage in a reciprocal and mutually beneficial relationship. When Eliade called the shaman the "master of the spirits," he was not implying "mastery over," but he explained that "the shaman controls his 'spirits' in the sense that he, a human being, is able to communicate with the dead, demons, and nature spirits, without thereby becoming their instrument."[3]

Although spirit allies can act in many capacities, there are generally three ways in which the shaman utilizes his or her ally or allies. These are:

1. As teacher. During the initiation, and whenever it is needed thereafter, the shaman undergoes training in shamanic techniques and practices under the guidance of a tutelary spirit. After recruiting the shamanic candidate, the tutelary

spirit instructs the neophyte in magical techniques, including special chants, healing practices, and communication in spirit language. In addition to *The Divine Comedy*, a more modern metaphor that we can look to is George Lucas's myth-inspired film *Star Wars* as an allegory of the shaman's journey and the strange cast of characters as the spirit allies that assist Luke Skywalker on his quest. The wise old sage Obe Wan Kenobi perfectly exemplifies the role of the tutelary spirit by unleashing the powers and possibilities that are inherent in his student but had before that time remained hidden from the world, and most of all from the student himself.

2. As guide. Without a guiding spirit to help navigate him or her through the unfamiliar terrain of the spirit realms, the shaman would be lost, unable to function within his journeys. As does the resourceful Han Solo, spirit guides know the customs of the lands, as well as how to cajole or converse with the locals to get what is needed. They also act in many cases as transportation to the other worlds, such as in Black Elk's vision of being carried to the upper realms by a bay horse or, in the case of Luke Skywalker, an old spaceship. These guides may assist the shaman in finding a client's lost soul, which may hide in any one of the three worlds. The spirit guide also makes sure that the shaman continues moving from one stage of the journey to the next, not getting stuck in a single moment or trapped by the emotion of the experience.

3. As protector. The overall job of these allies is to keep its charge healthy and safe. Protective spirits act as a kind of "spiritual bodyguard," protecting

the shaman from destructive forces that would cause harm to the shaman or to the patient. In *Star Wars*, hairy, animal-like Chewbacca didn't say much other than a few grunts and howls, but he was always on hand to clobber some obstructing force over the head so that they could continue on their mission. The protecting spirit guides help the shaman confront the obstacles that stand in the way of carrying out the work that needs to be done.

In the cases of Dante and Luke Skywalker, without this assistance the journey would likely not have gone past the first step. Dante might have been stuck in that dark forest for all eternity, and Luke Skywalker might never have left the planet Tatooine. The shaman must likewise develop a family of spirit allies to help him or her realize the goals of his or her quests. To try to enter into this world alone and without help is neither practical nor possible. Therefore, writes Malidoma Somé in *The Healing Wisdom of Africa*, "Among the Dagara, one can say to the healer, 'Teach me what you know'; but the better request to make the healer is, 'Teach me about what teaches you.'"[4]

From the One Comes Many

Before continuing on with this discussion of spirits, I think it is important to make an important distinction in language—that is, the difference between "spirit" (small "s") and "Spirit" (big "s"). Although shamanic philosophy is one of animism, in which everything that exists in both the seen and unseen world has its own spirit or soul, most traditions agree that this does not exclude the existence of one great singular creative power of the cosmos. In shamanic philosophy, these spiritual intelligences that exist everywhere and in everything all emanate from one creative source, called "Great Spirit" by some traditions, "God" in others, and a thousand other names. Everything in the universe is pervaded by this creative essence that funnels down from this one Source, uniting everything as one and making up the great web of life. This "supernatural electricity" is called by different names according to each tradition: *mana*, *mulunga*, and *orenda* from the Polynesian, African, and Native American native traditions, respectively. In *Star Wars*, George Lucas called it "The Force."

Rabbi Gershon Winkler of the Jewish shamanic tradition told me:

> In the mystical tradition of our people, every tree is alive because there's a spirit that is manifesting it. However, where we draw the line in our pantheism is that, while we believe that all things—from stones to stars to trees to people—are being spiraled into existence by their own individual spirits, we do not believe that these spirits are *the* Source. Instead, they are empowered by *Elohim*, which is the name we have for God. Literally, Elohim means "Source of Powers."… We believe that there's one Source of all powers, whether it is for better or for worse, and that everything else is an intermediary or a messenger or manifestation of that source in the physical world.[5]

As intermediaries, the intelligences of the spirit world are essential in providing the shaman with insights into the universal condition in a way that can be used in his or her work.

Sandra Ingerman, author of *Soul Retrieval*, had three near-death experiences as her initiatory calling into shamanic work. She says:

> When I had my near death experiences, I went to what I consider to be "God." And God is just complete love. For me, that was my experience. He gave me exactly the same amount of love as he would give a murderer standing next to me. I was not an individual. There was no separation. In terms of healing work, though, I find I can't really go to God or the Divine

Force and say, "I'm having a problem with this client, could you help me?" because all I would get back is love. Which is wonderful, but I need more practical advice like "Ok, this person needs to change their diet." Whereas, through the spirits who are the intermediaries of that power of the universe and that oneness, I can get that kind of practical, direct information.[6]

In his or her work, the shaman journeys to any of the three worlds to meet with these intelligences. As with all things encountered on the journey into non-ordinary reality, the form that these allies take is based upon each individual's personal symbol system. Free from time and space, there is an unlimited potential for individual expression and will translate into whatever form the individual can best relate to. Our personal taste, our cultural contexts, and our expectations play heavily into the form that these allies take. In *The Inferno*, the narrator, Dante, is portrayed as being a poet. Because of his own personal interests, he perceives his guide to be in the form of Virgil, a famous poet, someone he has respected and admired and in whom he can feel complete trust and faith. These associations are also not limited to physical forms. Some practitioners identify their spirit allies as sensations, such as scents or smells or emotional and physical feelings. Most likely, the "true" nature of our spirit allies, if indeed there is one, is one that our minds do not have a space for. Therefore they need to come to us in the way that our mind can translate and work with.

Despite the significance of a personal and cultural system involved in this, many forms that allies take, such as images of animals, nature spirits, various deities, and ancestors, are ones that remain consistent in almost every tradition across the globe. Perhaps these consistencies reflect those archetypal patterns that are recognized by our collective souls and from which come the images that form the shaman's pantheon of spirit allies.

Spirit Allies of the Middle World[7]

Some of the most useful allies that the shaman has are those that manifest in the Middle World, the realm of ordinary reality. For the shaman, the physical aspect of these manifestations that we encounter every day is only a small portion of the totality that is the physical world. Hidden behind the illusory veil of matter is the spirit that shapes and maintains its physical form. In the Hebrew language, in fact, the word for the physical universe is *olam*, which means "concealed," or that which is concealed within creation. A fundamental principle in shamanism is the concept that everything that exists in the three-dimensional realm contains its own spirit, its own consciousness. Plants, animals, stars, rivers, mountains, planet Earth, and even human-made objects, such as buildings and computers, are believed to have their own innate intelligence. This idea of spirit-in-all-things goes even further to include intangible manifestations of the Middle World such as the four cardinal directions, as well as all natural phenomena.

For most of us, that which exists is often so well disguised that we do not notice it beyond its physical appearance. For shamanic cultures living close to nature, however, creating and maintaining good relationships with these forces of the spirit world is essential to survival. If a hunt does not go well, if the crops fail, or if a storm or natural catastrophe falls upon them, it is believed that the spirits of these forces have been offended and must be appeased. If not, the entire community will be at risk. Proper conduct is essential in dealing with these unseen forces, and because of this a great part of the shaman's practice involves constant negotiations with the spirits of the land on which he or she lives. Jungle shamans of the Amazon have a deep connection to the spirits of plants, whereas those that live in the Andes work primarily with mountain spirits. Sacred sites upon the land are considered by the Huichols to be "dreaming gods and goddesses,"[8] and ceremonies and rituals are made throughout the year to honor the spirits of these places. This is as true in an urban environment as anywhere else. There are nature spirits everywhere, no matter how covered over in cement the land they live on might be. Although this may seem like an archaic belief system to those of us living in a scientifically rational, technologically based world, we all stand in awe of the natural world. No matter how hard we try to believe that we are immune from nature and its influences, we are still very much at the mercy of the forces of the natural world—forces that take very little mind of our own desires and that are still very much out of our conscious control.

Besides the spirit intrinsic within each object, place, or phenomena, within the natural world exist spiritual entities that watch over the totality of the physical world. From tradition to tradition, these nature spirits are given different personifications as well as varying roles and functions within the natural world. These entities go by different names: *fairies* in the Celtic tradition, *kontomble* to the people of the African Dagara tradition, and *auki* in the Peruvian shamanic tradition. These entities act as maintainers and advocates of the natural world. As representative for his community, the shaman is given the task of interacting with these forces to restore proper harmony between the community and the mysterious powers of nature.

In my talks with shamans who work within the various traditions around the world, I have noticed that many have similar ways of referring to the manner in which the shaman interacts with the forces of nature to ensure this balance. For example, Tom Cowan told me:

> According to the Christian tradition, angels were created to praise and celebrate the power and the beauty of God in Heaven. One theory about the fairies is that they were created to do that on Earth—to celebrate and praise the goodness, love, and yearning of God in

nature. So if you shapeshift your soul enough to become the goodness, love, and yearning of, say, a waterfall, or tree, or a moss-covered stone, then the fairies see you as something they should praise and celebrate.... If you can change your consciousness to become the consciousness of the world of nature, the fairies will make themselves known to you.[9]

In the Hawaiian tradition of *kahuna* shamanism, a similar technique of transforming consciousness in order to interact with the natural world is used, called *grokking*.[10] "We use this technique on things like storms," says *kahuna* shaman Serge Kahili King. "If there is a big storm coming towards us that we know will be very destructive, we would identify deeply with the storm. As the storm, we become aware of the storm's potential, the ways it could go, and then pick a direction that is least destructive."[11]

Erik Gonzalez of the Mayan tradition describes a similar merging. He says:

When someone asks the medicine person, "How did you learn how to mix these plant medicines to create this effect?" we say, "The plants talk to us." When we smoke our pipes, we take the herb that came from the Earth and we smoke it so that it will go into our system and interact with us at a cellular level, at a conscious level, and at a subconscious level.... This is how we learned to move the energy that is needed to create a condition that we want.... You can become, let's say, a molecule of water. Suddenly you know what it is feeling, what it is thinking when it is the morning dew. You become that molecule—you start seeing and hearing and feeling and knowing the collective aspect of the water in all its moments of being, such as when it is falling down from the sky, becoming denser and denser until it freezes into an icicle.[12]

But, I asked him, how will becoming a drop of water help us?

"If you are one with the water, then you can communicate with the lightning and the thunder and rain and the clouds and create what you need," he told me. "It's like with the aborigine people of Australia. The outside world says, 'How can they live in that desolate place? How can they find water?' Well, if you ask them, they say, 'The water talks to us.' They dream the water. The water's energies are flowing through them."

For centuries, the western world has sought to harness and control the forces of nature, often to our own peril. In contrast, the shaman's way of working is more like a humble joining with the spirits of nature, a mergence of two great forces. In their ecstasies, the shaman merges into oneness with these spirits in order to help maintain this balance and bring change that is most beneficial to the community.

Spirit Allies of Non-Ordinary Reality

Besides those manifesting in physical form in the Middle World, the shaman's pantheon is made up of numerous allies that exist solely in non-ordinary reality. Communications with these allies take place during the shaman's ecstatic journeys into the various spirit realms. Despite some variances, the forms that these allies take within these journeys remain remarkably consistent throughout a variety of individual and cultural experiences. These include power animals, ancestors, and a variety of gods and goddesses manifesting from the mythology from each individual culture.

Spirit Allies of the Lower World

Of all the spirit allies that are said to reveal themselves to the shaman within the context of the Lower Worlds, power animals stand out as the most common inhabitants of these realms. However, although I concentrate on power animals in this section, I want to be clear that the Lower World can be the residence of any number and form of spirit allies.

Power Animals

Power animals[13] are viewed as the most sacred of allies by many, if not all, of the shamanic traditions around the world and hold a special place in the shaman's pantheon of spirit allies. Just as many western religions believe that everyone has a guardian angel, most shamanic traditions believe that every person is imbued with power stemming from his or her animal ally.

Although the shaman may make contact with the spirits of certain animals residing in the Middle World, such as in the practice of hunting magic, these Middle World spirits do not usually act as power sources for the shaman. Nor do they typically act as guides throughout his or her journeys. There are exceptions, of course, but this is my general understanding of it. On the other hand, power animals (and other non-physically manifested spirits that we will look at) function as personal guardians and mentors to the shaman, relating to him or her in a kind of working partnership. In addition, animals that are extinct or mythological in ordinary reality, such as dinosaurs and unicorns, are potential allies within the realm of spirit.

Judging by the ancient cave paintings from around the world that contain depictions of animals and the "shamans" that desired to transform into them, this reverence for animals spans back many thousands of years to Paleolithic times. But what is it about animals that captivates the attention of the psyche and makes them so important to the shaman and to mythmakers around the world?

Of all the non-human forms that exist, animals are our closest hereditary allies, sharing with us a common universal animal ancestor. Sometime around 1 billion years ago, the first animals—of which humankind is one—began to evolve out from our ancient predecessors that crept out of the primordial ooze. When, as many traditions do, we call animals our "brothers and sisters," we are acknowledging that common ancestry, recalling a period of time when our species wore feathers and fur and, as animals do today, lived in absolute harmony and balance in the cosmos. Somewhere along the evolutionary line, the human animal developed a capacity for self-reflection that—so far as we know—is unique to our species and, for better and for worse, runs a system of checks and balances against our natural animal instincts. Of course we don't know for sure, but chances are that the lion is not lying around the Savannah thinking, "What is my place in the universe?" Imagine the horror of the first existential "I" thought of our primeval ancestor that stopped suddenly in the middle of foraging food, looked down at its handful of berries, and thought, "What is the meaning of life?"

This evolutionary split in consciousness is reflected in the myths of tribal people, who tell stories of a time when animals and people shared a common language and were able to speak freely with each other and with the spirit world. The shaman's initiation—and subsequent journeys—involve the placing aside of this "I" state in order to re-discover his or her animal nature.

"Each time a shaman succeeds in sharing in the animal mode of being," says Eliade in *Shamanism*, "he in a manner re-establishes the situation that existed *in illo tempore*, in mythical times, when the divorce between man and the animal world had not yet occurred."[14]

Unlike human beings, animals have never lost their natural instincts or intrinsic knowledge of how to act in harmony with the universe. When food supplies become scarce, an intrinsic knowing tells them to stop breeding in order to conserve resources. I have heard that kangaroos even have the ability to hold a developing fetus in a state of suspended animation, stopping its growth until such time as conditions improve and there are sufficient resources to sustain another life. Animals carry no shadow, no guilt, no doubt. Their existence is based purely on instinct. Human beings, however, burdened and blessed with an ego mind that gets in the way of our own innate wisdom, must continually seek to reconnect to the part of ourselves that will always remain in harmony with the universe.

Because of this, many shamanic traditions believe that the pathway to the spirit world can be reached only with the help of animal assistants.[15,16] Some also believe that not only does the shaman need help from his or her animal ally, but, in order to reach the outer worlds, he or she must learn to *transform* into them as well.

This transformation can occur on a number of different levels. Some individuals, it has been said, can make a cellular transformation, a physical shapeshift from human to animal form. Across the world, legends abound about individuals who can change into animal form at will, including the werewolves of European folklore, the leopard man of Africa, the werejaguars of South America, and the shark shamans of the Pacific atolls.[17]

More typically, however, the shift is not evident on the physical level, but instead involves a dramatic transformation of the shaman's psyche and consciousness. Because of human beings' close affiliation with the animal world, the human soul, one's essence, is said to change easily from human into beast. During ceremony, the shaman typically embodies his or her power animal, including wearing clothing made out of its skin or feathers, making animal sounds, and otherwise mimicking its behavior. Each animal holds an archetypal essence representing certain strengths and powers that the shaman may need to utilize during his or her journey. By merging with the animal ally, the shaman takes on those attributes that are needed during the course of his or her journey. This is reminiscent of the beserkers of Scandinavia, who would take on the essence of Bear in order to go more ferociously into battle. Merging with the spirit of Jaguar will help the shaman travel quickly over long distances. Taking on the psychic impression of Eagle can help him or her ascend quickly to the Upper World or, as

Snake, descend into the Lower World. If the shaman is in need of courage in order to undergo a physical or emotional transformation, Butterfly may assist him or her as guardian and guide. All animals are respected for their particular strengths and characteristics; no animal is considered less significant than any other. I once heard a story about a shaman who called upon the spirit of Lice because of their ability to consume dead matter.

Once the shaman becomes aligned with a particular power animal or animals, he or she can take on the qualities of that animal, its personality, in order to confront the challenges needed on its journey. The power animal and the shaman thus merge to become one entity, with the animal's particular strengths and attributes filling in the spaces where the shaman's own weaknesses leave him or her open and exposed. It is believed in many traditions that if the power animal deserts the individual, the person loses that strength and vital essence. The power animal's abandonment furthermore leaves the person with open spaces that can be filled with negative spirits bringing disease and misfortune. As Jung said, "The acceptance of the animal soul is the condition for wholeness and a fully lived life."

Spirit Allies of the Upper World

The Upper Worlds are commonly considered the realm of "light beings," those spirits and entities that guide us on our quest for greater conscious awareness and enlightenment. Besides the obvious association with the Creator God of various traditions, the Upper World is considered to be the home of a variety of spirit allies that make themselves available to the shaman, including cultural deities, ancestors, ascended masters, and angelic beings. From their place in the sky realm, these allies in the Upper Worlds are able to see the universe in a way that those of us in the physical world are unable: in its totality. Existing in a realm unrestrained by time and space, Upper World allies can look into the past and future and describe it as easily as we could the present, perceiving how all actions influence each other, making up an inseparable whole. Just as Lower World allies bring us back to our base, animal nature, spirit guides of the Upper World are so useful to the shaman because they represent our greatest potential for growth.

Cultural Deities

Almost every shamanic culture from around the world has a rich *dramatis personae* of gods and goddesses from whom they draw power and meaning during their ceremonies. From tradition to tradition, these divine beings are recognized as the figureheads behind both the darker and lighter aspects of the universe, manipulating and controlling the emotional sensibilities of humankind and ruling over the forces of nature and of man. Still today most, if not all, traditions of shamanism maintain their own pantheon of gods and goddesses whom they call upon to assist them in their work.

Because of this close affiliation with human impulses, the gods and goddesses of old have been likened to Jung's archetypes, a family of characters representing distinct aspects of the unconscious personality that makes up the total psyche of the individual. Each one of us contains the rage of Hera, the beauty and sensuality of Lakshmi, the propensity for chaos and destruction of Loki, and the innocence of Persephone. The gods of old—warrior, trickster, mother, sacred cannibal—manifest both in the universe and in the inner workings of humankind. Some believe that, as a way of acknowledging these persisting archetypes, the ancients isolated these characteristics and created a pantheon of gods and goddesses to act as representative of each.

Still, embarking upon the path of shamanism does not necessarily mean a return to the period in which one believed that his thoughts came to him from gods and were not internally generated. On the contrary. The gods and spirits do not take the place of personal identity or consciousness but mirror in a perfect model of "as within, so without."

Ancestors and Ascended Masters

In his or her ecstasies, the shaman travels to the realms beyond death, down a path blazed by those who have died and traveled it previously. In shamanic cultures, death is not seen as an end to everything, but a shapeshift that the soul makes from one thing to another. Shamans often feel connected to those who have lived before and rely on their ancestors to watch over them and give them guidance. Because of this, the shaman's ally often appears as the spirit of someone who once lived in the physical realm but who, by having left physical form, now resides in the spirit world and is therefore accessible to the shaman in his or her work. These are not to be confused with ghosts, which are the spirits or souls of people who are trapped between the worlds—usually by their own corporeal attachments—and are unable to make the journey to the realms beyond death. These can often cause trouble in the physical world. According to the Siberian and Mongolian traditions, the human soul consists of multiple parts, each of which has a different fate after death. One part of the soul, called *suld* or *unen fayenga*, is said to remain on earth, existing as an ancestral spirit and watching over its descendants. The soul remains this way for several generations until it leaves to live in a place in nature, such as trees or waterfalls and the like. Even then, the spirit may still be called upon if needed.[18]

Although the term *ancestor* generally refers to individuals connected through blood lineage, it can also refer to the spirits of those who have shared a common goal as the shaman, such as Dante's encountering his deceased mentor, the great poet Virgil. Those who desire to walk down a certain spiritual path, for example, may find themselves coming face to face with Jesus Christ, Buddha, and any other variety of saints and ascended masters whose souls have become elevated to the role of spirit teachers through their service in the physical realm. Unlike those spirit allies that have never existed in physical form, these beings have an understanding of the experience of having a physical body and can therefore provide certain insights that other spirit allies might not. In ritual, the shaman very often appeals to his or her ancestors for guidance, knowing that if he or she does not, catastrophe may occur. Ancestors represent a great chain of wisdom that the shaman may tap into. Each generation stands upon the shoulders of the last, creating a ladder reaching up to the heavens. In some traditions, ancestor spirits are responsible for recruiting new shamans and passing down the wisdom of their lineage.

As well as those who have lived in the past, I have heard shamans talk about meeting with spirit allies who have not yet lived in physical form but who will do so at some point in the future.

Angelic Beings

Spirit allies of the upper realms can also take the form of ethereal or angelic beings. During a particularly difficult time of my life several years ago, I went to do some journeying work with two wonderful shamanic practitioners. I was completely strung out emotionally, at my wit's end, and one of them told me I needed to get in touch with my allies in the Upper Worlds. One of the practitioners verbally led me into the Upper World. As she described it to me, I followed along in my mind's eye. In this vision, I stood in a large, light-filled dome, surrounded by dozens of very tall beings, their faces hidden behind the hoods of long silver robes. The beings took no notice of my presence, even though several of them were close enough to touch. These beings are holding scrolls, she told me, and on them are the answers to any question I might ask. With awe, I held my breath, waiting to hear what great wisdom they would give to me. At that moment, the being standing nearest to me turned its head. It had the face of an old man; it was gaunt and skeletal, but radiantly healthy. He leaned towards me with a mischievous smile. "Actually," he said, winking, "it's the ingredients for Fruit Loops."

I laughed so hard that I nearly broke right out of the journey. Not that it mattered to me. Whatever "answer" I could benefit from whatever was written on the scrolls was unimportant. Life had become too serious in the past few months. What I had really needed was not answers but a good laugh, a little irreverence to jolt me into a new perspective. As do human beings, spirit allies all have their own distinct personalities. Some are serious; some, as in that case, use their sense of humor as a healing tool. Allies can be aloof or extremely attentive, but all have the best intentions for their charge.

Much in the same way that the shaman merges with the essence of his power animal or with a particular force in the natural world, the experience of interacting with allies from these Upper World realms can involve a similar kind of mergence. Often the shaman is said to enter into a "spirit marriage," in which he or she enters into a sexual relationship with certain spirit beings, often his or her tutelary spirit.[19] These divine unions often include the shaman having children in the other realms with the spirit mate. These children, it seems, are the result of a blending of the two worlds, spirit and physical, much as in the story of the conception of Christ.

In his or her journeys into ecstasy, the shaman relies on these spirit allies to help navigate through the realms of spirit. These spirit allies may remain with the shaman throughout the course of a lifetime depending on the shaman's needs and as long as the relationship remains respectful. Sometimes an ally will leave the shaman and be replaced with a new form that will allow the shaman to increase his or her education and power. Although all people have spirit allies whether they know it or not, the shaman, by nature of his or her work, has a greater responsibility for maintaining good relationships with his or her spirit allies. In return, the spirit allies will provide the shaman with wisdom and power not normally accessible to those in the physical realm.

Spirits of the Unmaking

In his or her journeys to the other worlds, the shaman may also encounter spirits of the "unmaking"—that is, spirits that wish to cause chaos and imbalance in the universe. Like the *formorians* of Celtic cosmology, these forces are not considered "bad" or "evil" but are manifestations of the one Creative Source that is itself a blend of both creative and destructive elements. Their presence can, however, be antithetical to the shaman's work, causing imbalance where the need is for balance, sickness where the desired condition is health. Besides establishing relationships with his or her spirit allies, the shaman must also become familiar with those spirits that may cause conflict in his or her practice. To be an effective healer, the shaman must learn to communicate and interact with these discordant energies, trick or overpower them, or, as a last resort, do battle with them in order to create the transformation that is desired.

The exact natures and identities of these spirits are as diverse as those of the shaman's allies. These spirits may be identified as ghosts or, as in the Tibetan tradition, the various soul parts of deceased humans who, having died from an unnatural death or not having had an appropriate funeral, become evil spirits. Some see these forces as being the shadow side of the cultural deities mentioned earlier: that is, they represent one of the two faces of God, this time the dark as opposed to the light. Behind the creative aspect of every deity is an equal and opposite propensity for destruction. An encounter with the gods is therefore not always a pleasant experience. In the Indian pantheon, for example, figures such as Rudra and Kali can be seen as personifications of the dark and wrathful faces of the divine. Even portions of Christianity depict God the Creator as at once both loving and merciful, jealous and vengeful. It is within this paradox that the universe assumes its form.

In the Jewish shamanic tradition, this darker aspect of the universe is called *Sit'ra Ach'ra*, which means, "The Other Side," or "That Which is Behind Us and That Which is After Us." Rabbi Gershon Winkler told me this about the *Sit'ra Ach'ra*:

> The *Sit'ra Ach'ra* is the black hole of the universe—the force that seeks to swallow up creation into the oneness of the Godhead again. In fact, the universe is swallowing itself into a big black hole all the time. This manifests in different ways: through people—as in the case of genocide—and through what we call natural occurrences, such as earthquakes and tornadoes. In itself, the *Sit'ra Ach'ra* is not evil. It is the part of the Creator that seeks to swallow everything whole, just as there's a part of the Creator that wants everyone to be themselves.
>
> This same desire is a part of every one of us as well. If you think about it in terms of a relationship, a part of me would love to swallow my wife whole and make her completely what *I* envision, what *I* want. But then there's the other part of me that is called *t'zimt'zum*, which means "stepping back." We step back to allow the other to be themselves. It's a dance.[20]

Malevolent spirits can also be brought into form by buildups of negative energy created by living beings, from a single person to an entire culture. As shamanic practitioner Alex Stark explains in "The Spirit World," an article from his Web site:

> In certain cases, obsessions, phobias, neuroses can assume such great strength that they become condensed into discrete energy forms that assume a life independent of any other attachments. These can clearly be dangerous, since they are the product of human minds, and can contain great potential for hate, rage, morbidity, and self-loathing, to mention a few. I remember one case in which an apparently healthy woman moved into a home where severely morbid woman had lived. Within months my client developed cancer and had to

undergo surgery for the removal of a lung. This started
her on a long search for the causes of her ailment. She
was tenacious, however and was able to launch herself
into the search with great vitality and intelligence. It
was my fortune to meet her and work on the morbid
feeling her house was transferring to her as part of her
strategy for healing. When the morbid feelings lifted,
she coincidentally began to recover.[21]

The idea that malevolent spirits are responsible for sick-
nesses of the body and mind may seem preposterous to the
"rational" mind. And yet, one must remember that when bi-
ologists first suggested that various microbes imperceptible to
the human eye caused disease, the scientific community responded with similar skepticism. In the western world, we all
fully accept the idea of positive and negative spirits—as long
as they are clothed in psychological or scientific lingo. Instead
of "angels" and "devils," we refer to them as "archetypes" and
"neuroses," though we do at times still refer to our own inner
trials and shadow parts as our "demons." We talk about having
a stroke of good or bad luck, as if these things existed outside of
ourselves, attaching themselves to us on a whim. Much of our
language about illness is the same as an indigenous person might
talk about sickness caused by malevolent forces. For example,
we talk of "fighting cancer" as if cancer were an adversarial spirit
to be battled.

When our physical immunity, our body's power system,
is down, we become susceptible to a host of bacteria and vi-
ruses that feed upon our sudden weakness. Just as any one of
us is sure to take various steps to remain as healthy as possible
in order to ward off sickness-causing germs, so too does the
shaman take various steps to keep these malevolent forces at
bay. By keeping relations with his or her spirit allies strong,
such as by doing daily practices to honor them, the shaman is
also able to stay strong enough to resist the influence of their
opposites. When a shaman disrespects or insults his or her

ally, the ally may abandon him or her, thereby leaving places of weakness within the shaman's energy field. This can be dangerous. As nature abhors a vacuum, these empty spaces can then be filled by these malicious entities that can wreck havoc on the shaman's physical, emotional, and spiritual capabilities. In order to maintain health and power, the shaman must carefully and respectfully cultivate the relationship with the spirits with which he or she is allied.

Over a period of time interacting with these forces, both malevolent and beneficial, the shaman will become familiar with their natures, their strengths and weaknesses, and the way in which even the most discordant of energies can be best utilized.

Patterns Emerging

This theme of the shaman merging consciousness with his or her spirit allies has emerged over and over again throughout the chapter, echoing itself even in the most diverse of traditions. As this idea implies, making a connection to the spirit realm involves not simply a transmission of power from the spirit ally to the shaman, but a blending of essences in order to acquire wisdom, strength, and ability. At the start of his journey into *The Inferno*, Dante says to Virgil, "From now, we two shall share one will together." Dante recognizes, just as the shaman does, that total unification with his guide is necessary in order to successfully navigate through the hostile terrain. Such a feat involves breaking down the barriers of consciousness, liberating the conscious imagination to such an extent that the individual can make that psychic leap from the ego mind to the transcendent part of the self that is always connected to the totality of the Divine Source. This ability to reconnect to this infinite oneness is an innate ability of every human being and opens up the possibility for dramatic changes to occur in both the physical and spiritual realms.

But how, practically, does the shaman make this switch in consciousness, this leap from one thing to another, a shapeshift of essence, or even of physical and cellular form? In the next chapter, we will take a look at how the shaman does just that: how the symbolic gestures of ritual and prayer—when used to their fullest extent—can have this kind of transforming effect upon consciousness and, ultimately, the soul of the individual.

Exercises

Exercise #11: Establishing a Relationship With Your Allies

In the previous exercises, you took journeys to the Lower, Upper, and Middle Worlds. Who or what were the allies that revealed themselves to you? What animals showed up in your journeys? What human forms? What attributes do these animals and/or people possess that may be beneficial for you to embody? In what way can they act as your guides? Do whatever research you need to in order to feel more connected to these allies. For example, if a historical figure such as Abraham Lincoln showed up, do some reading about and research into his life. What do his actions symbolize to you? If an animal presented itself to you, find out more about its habits. What medicine does it bring to you? What teachings? Do the same for any being that may have made itself known to you during the journey. This can include any "negative" entities—that is, beings that may have caused you some anxiousness or fear when you first met them on your journey. What is your sense of a message, if any? Record your findings and move on.

Exercise #12: Symbolizing Your Allies

Find representations of your spirit allies. This can include photos of ancestors and mentors, statues of gods and goddesses, animal skins or bone, figurines—whatever images make you feel connected to your allies. Just collect them for now; we will work with them later on.

Chapter 5

Dialogue With the Sacred: Ritual Magic

J n the previous chapter, we explored the significance of the shaman in his or her work undergoing a kind of shapeshift, a transformation of consciousness in which he or she establishes an energetic resonance with any number of spirit allies and/or forces of nature. Having learned to transcend the ego mind for the duration of the ecstatic experience, the shaman is able to establish a state of oneness with all forms of existence (both spiritual and physical) to the extent that he or she is able to merge consciousness with those forms. As we have seen, the ecstatic process is viewed differently in various traditions. In some, such as the Tibetan and Korean shamanic practices, the experience is described as an "incoming," such as cases of intentional possession in which the tutelary spirit is said to inhabit the shaman's body for the duration of ecstasy. In others, it is seen as an "outgoing," in which the shaman's soul is thought to leave his or her body and travel outwards into the various spiritual dimensions.

This idea of the shaman's *mergence* with the spirit world, however, could be seen as reconciling these two seemingly contradictory descriptions of the ecstatic process. Viewed in this light, the experience is neither one of going out nor of coming in (though perhaps it could be described as both), but rather a coming together of two forms of consciousness into one all-encompassing whole. If we go back to the idea proposed in Chapter 1—that the shaman's levels of reality resemble a stew rather than layers of the cake (and that levels we perceive are but constructs of our minds)—the ecstatic process becomes a way of temporarily eradicating the boundaries set up by our limited consciousness, allowing these various energies to come together as one. Now that we have explored the personal encounters that the shaman has within these states of consciousness, it is now time to look at the stage that is set for the shaman to bring these experiences to a community level—that is, through the process of ritual.

Ritual is an essential part of every tradition, as it is the principal method used by shamans to create a dialogue with the unseen world in order to restore balance and bring about transformation within the physical world. In this chapter, we will explore this ecstatic process of mergence further and see how the state of being achieved in ritual can create dramatic transformation in the physical world on a personal, community, and planetary level.

The Transformative Power of Ritual and Prayer

The process of ritual as a way of transforming consciousness has a place in every culture across the world and in every religion or spirituality known to humankind. Although the resulting transformation may be subtle in some cases, and therefore more difficult to see, even non-shamanic spiritual traditions that do not employ the use of obvious outward stimuli—hallucinogens, drumming, or chanting—have ways of transforming the consciousness of the ritual participant. The symbolic eating and drinking of the body and blood of Christ by ingesting bread and wine has a profound effect upon the mindset in the moment of Holy Communion in Catholic Mass, which, as the word signifies, also involves a "coming together of" or "harmony with" the holy spirit.

Unlike those of some other religions and spiritualities, the rituals of shamanic societies are undertaken not just as means of passive worship of the Creative Spirit and its lesser deities, although forms of worship *are* involved. Instead, ritual is used as a way of restoring the natural balance between spirit and flesh in a way that all participants walk away from the ceremonies healed and transformed.[1] The transformative power of ritual is so significant that in tribal communities when things are believed to be out of balance (manifesting in sickness or any form of instability), all of village life is suspended until the prescribed rituals are done.[2] This sense of urgency stems from the belief that the spirit world and physical world are so intertwined that if something in the physical world is experiencing imbalance, it is a sign that the spirit world is out of balance as well. The shaman guides the participants through the sacred act of ritual, a realm that transcends both time and space, in order to restore balance to situations that need healing. In this context, ritual becomes not just a habit or diversion, but a way of establishing a necessary dialogue with the unseen realms, a communication that is essential for the life and health of the community and individual.

As the mediator between the realms, the shaman is responsible for establishing and maintaining this connection throughout the duration of the ceremony. As the spirit allies guide the shaman, the shaman in turn guides his or her community through the physical embodiment of a living myth—a journey into the world of spirit made familiar to the shaman through his or her repeated visits to the other worlds. In ritual, the shaman brings these mythic visions home and turns them into physical experiences that all individuals can participate in.

Although during his or her journeys the shaman removes his or her consciousness from the physical realm and enters into the spiritual plane, ritual is a way of taking those experiences and bringing them back to the physical through movement and symbolic gesture. Throughout the ritual, the shaman establishes and maintains a protected container in which the participants can engage in a safe exchange with the invisible world. Although the shaman acts much like a priest during the process, his or her role is not one of didactic instruction. His or her function remains that of a bridge between the realms that others may use to pass over to have their own direct revelation from the spirit realm.

The 5 Stages of Ritual

Margot Adler reports in *Drawing Down the Moon* that in his classic text, *Real Magic*, Isaac Bonewits defined ritual as "any ordered sequence of events or actions, including directed thoughts, especially one that is repeated in the same manner each time, and that is designed to produce a predictable altered state of consciousness within which certain magical or religious results may be obtained."[3] Ritual is much like a language, a language that reflects the particular beliefs and needs of any given culture. Every tradition expresses itself in its own distinct forms of ritual, from the sweat lodges of Native American traditions to the Dagara Dagger of Fire ritual. This expression permeates every aspect of the ritual process, from the shaman's costume to the design of the ceremonial space, as well as the various power objects used to help facilitate communications with the unseen worlds.

Certain consistent patterns do still emerge within the "ordered sequence of events" that Bonewits described. Many rituals, from both shamanic and non-shamanic traditions, follow a similar process that once again can be seen as mirroring the five stages of the shaman's initiation, beginning with the Calling phase through to the shaman's final return to the profane.

Although the initiatory experience involves a symbolic, psychological, and sometimes even physical death and rebirth of the shaman alone, ritual re-creates this experience on a community level, as well as on the cosmic level, providing the space for the mythic reenactment of the creation of the universe and the life of the individual.

The Calling to and Preparation of Sacred Space

Rituals may be embarked upon for a number of reasons. Ceremonies may be undertaken as a way of creating a specific transformation that is needed, but that is beyond the ability to effect by ordinary means such as the healing of the individual or community, protection, hunting, or weather magic—just to name a few. Some rituals have a more prophylactic function, such as the daily practices used to maintain a healthy relationship between the shaman and his or her spirit helpers. Other rituals mark significant passages such as the cycles of nature, the phases of the moon, and seasons, as well as the cycles of human life, as in birth, puberty, marriage, and death rites. Rituals may be executed by a single individual alone; others involve an entire community of people brought together by a common goal. Some may range from simple gestures of intent and prayer; others may last several days on end.

Whatever the form the ritual takes, a goal and intention are made clear to those who will be participating. Preparations to enter the ritual space may include any personal requirements that the participant is asked to make, such as abstaining from food, sex, and/or other "taboo" substances in the days preceding the ritual. This, as well as bathing or other kinds of cleansing, ensures that the participants will come to the space in as "pure" a state as possible. This preparation is also a means of directing a personal or communal focus on the intent behind the ritual. This begins the process of moving the participant's consciousness and focus away from the habitual physical and mental patterns of mundane life, readying them for communion with the spirit realms.

As the participants prepare themselves, the ritual space is likewise prepared. The arrangement and design of the ceremonial space play a significant role in the enactment of ritual. All rituals, on one level or another, from the most subtle to the most profound, are at the core a reenactment of the myth of the creation of the cosmos, lending an outer form to the cosmology of that particular spiritual tradition. In the Tamang tradition, ritual re-creates the long gone "Truth Era," a time long ago when humans were immortal, as the gods are, and able to travel freely and easily between the worlds. Because of an act of deception, the pathway between Heaven and Earth was severed.[4]

Within every ritual there is a point of focus, a place where all intent is directed, such as an altar, fire, or staff.[5] This point of focus is viewed as a symbolic representation of the axis mundi, the navel of the world from which the universe births itself over and over again and the place where all communication to the spirit world takes place. Participants use the focal point much as they do a telephone: as a means of accessing and dialoguing with the spirit realms.

The design of the ritual space often further mimics the cosmic sphere by including representations of the four directions, along with their corresponding elements and attributes. In this way, the directions and their elements act as the spiritual horizon, the container to hold and protect the energy that will be created during the ceremony. This circular space acts as the wheel of the cosmos, with the axis mundi as its stable and stationary hub. The circle as a symbol represents that which is without beginning or end, as in the cycles of death and rebirth. The destruction myths of shamanic traditions never imply an eternal end. What follows the great apocalypses in these stories is always a rebirth into a new form. The Scandinavian myth of Ragnarok, known as the "Twilight of the Gods," describes a time (sometimes described as a past event, other times as prophesy of events to come) when the forces of destruction and chaos will be unleashed and destroy Asgard, the world of the gods, and Midgard, "Middle Earth," home of humankind. Two, however—a man and a woman— will survive this upheaval by hiding within the trunk of Yggdrasil, the World Tree. As in ritual, destruction of the old must take place so that so that something new can begin.

The cosmos is enormous, greater than our human minds can grasp, and therefore overwhelming from our perspective on the earth plane. Within the ritual space the cosmos is re-built on a microcosmic scale—one that can be connected to with relative ease—so that the shaman and participants may work with it on a practical level. In creating this blueprint of the cosmos, the participants themselves become as gods, able to engage with and manipulate the subtle energies invoked within the space.

The shaman him or herself often becomes a miniature cos-mos as well, reflected in the costumes that he or she wears during the ceremony. In the Tamang tradition of Tibet, sha-mans wear headdresses made of peacock feathers and long red and white scarves, representing the Rainbow Bridge that con-nects Earth with Heaven. These symbols are said to reflect the shaman's ability to travel to the various realms as well as aid them in the magical flights.[6] Likewise, shamans will also often wear masks that represent animals or various gods and de-mons, as well as the skins of animals that they wish to em-body. In this same way, the shaman's costume acts as an aid in his or her journey into ecstasy.

Both the shaman and the ritual space are often further equipped with an altar containing various tools and power objects. These include natural objects such as rocks and shells, representations of the elements and directions, totems, reli-gious objects such as cultural deities, and the like. These ob-jects act as representations of the invisible sacred, symbolic manifestations of the various aspects of the divine that can be harnessed within the object and utilized within the ceremony. Again, an example of this is the mesa of many South American traditions, a cloth altar upon which various power objects are placed, representing the cosmic opposition between order and chaos and all other aspects of the universal condition. I was once told the story of a Peruvian shaman who even included a Tasmanian Devil Pez dispenser on his mesa because he "liked its wild energy." As the community needs the shaman to help them connect with the unseen realms, the shaman needs assistance from these tools to stimulate power and alter perceptions, helping the shaman make a magical connection between the participants and the divine worlds.

Invocation and Purification

Once sacred space has been constructed and designed, once the participants are gathered, and the focus of intent and purpose has been established, the ritual is ready to begin. Most, if not all, shamanic ceremonies begin with the shaman calling forth his or her spirit allies, as well as further constructing the boundaries of sacred space by invoking the four directions and the attributes and elements associated with each.[7] This invocation often includes appeals to the spirit of the earth and the spirits of the celestial realm such as the sun, moon, stars, and Great Creator Spirit. The summoning of the four directions, earth, and sky is a way for the shaman to both reconstruct the cosmic sphere and establish a safe, contained space that is well-protected from any negative spirits or energies. Because of this, the shaman must be very specific as to which spirits are to be invited into the ritual space, so as not to allow any unwelcome spirits in. Keeping the ritual space safe and fluid is the prime directive of the shaman in this work, for it is essential that the participants feel safe and protected as they open themselves up to a mergence with the sacred.

The invocation is a time for the shaman to send out his or her prayers, to formally invite the spirit allies to join the circle and assist them in their work. This statement of purpose also aids in making the visualization and intent of each ritual participant the same (if there is more than one), creating a focus of consciousness that goes beyond the personal, thereby achieving a resonance within the group's intent. By establishing this cohesiveness and harmony of consciousness, the group merges first with one another before entering into mergence with the divine.

In his book, *Inner Work*, Jungian analyst Robert A. Johnson praised ritual for its ability to create awe and reverence in a human being for something outside of him or herself, citing it as a significant contribution to the psychological health of an individual:

> All my experience as a psychologist leads me to the conclusion that a sense of *reverence* is necessary for psychological health. If a person has no sense of reverence, no feeling that there is anyone or anything that inspires awe, it generally indicates an ego inflation that cuts the conscious personality off completely from the nourishing springs of the unconscious. It is ironic, then, that so much of our modern culture is aimed at eradicating all reverence, all respect for the high truths and qualities that inspire a feeling of awe and worship in the human soul.[8]

Indigenous people know that physical reality is complete only with the presence of spirit, and therefore ritual becomes a synthesis, a merging of the two normally separate realities. Because of this, the invocation is stated carefully, as it is an expression of reverence and interdependence.

Purification of the Ego

The reenactment of this mythic moment of creation during ritual allows for regeneration of both cosmos and individual.

By retracing the steps of creation back to its primordial beginnings, the individual likewise is able to undergo a kind of symbolic rebirth in which he or she returns to the state of purity of that newborn child. Just as the purification stage in the initiation involves an annihilation of the ego, in this stage of ritual the shaman and the participants place the ego and all its shadow parts off to the side in order to enter into transcendence. As Brant Secunda told me:

> One of the objectives or goals of having ceremonies is to get one into that "perfect" ecstatic state—to be able to leave your imperfections behind, at least for the duration of the ceremony. The Huichols say that it is important to act in a good way, and that trying hard is the most important thing. But shamans are just normal people. They make mistakes like everyone else. The difference is that there's no Heaven or Hell in the Huichol cosmology. If a Huichol does something wrong, he or she can absolve themselves of it through doing a ceremony to help them start anew.[9]

Purification often involves an energetic cleansing using any one or more of the four elements, such as the smoke of aromatic plants such as sage or water from sacred wells as in the Celtic tradition. To further purge themselves, participants may utilize any one or more of the techniques for going into altered states described in the journeying chapter, allowing their ego mind to be overwhelmed and overpowered by spirit. During this stage, the shaman often begins to dance his or her power animal, mimicking the animal's movements and habits, churning him or herself into a state of ecstasy and resonance.

Sandra Ingerman explained it to me this way:

> In order to be a good spiritual healer, you have to bring spirit through your body. If you're in a real ego state of consciousness, there's no room for spirit to move through you to do the work. In indigenous societies,

this is where the shaman's dances and songs come in. Being able to dance and sing helps move the ego out of the way so that the power of the universe can come through the shaman. If you watch shamans working, they dance and sing for hours before doing their work! Some indigenous cultures down in South America use vision plants, which totally blast the ego. That's where the miracles happen.... Dealing with the ego is a constant struggle, but as a shamanic practitioner you can't stop working on yourself, because practitioners who don't work on themselves are usually not of great help to other people.[10]

Illumination and Mergence

Once purification of the ego self has been achieved, the shaman and ritual participants enter into ecstasy and, therefore, the phase of ritual that is the place of the highest and most dramatic change in consciousness takes place. This state, as in the stage of mergence during initiation, has been described as a fusion of the individual and that of the divine spirit:

> Ecstasy is literally a departure from, a tearing away from, or surpassing of the human limitations and also a meeting with and embracing of the divine. It is a fusion of being with being, in which the mystic experiences a union that he characterizes as a nuptial union: "God is in me and I am in him." The mystic experiences God himself in an inexpressible encounter because it is beyond the ordinary experience of man.[11]

Some have described this feeling as that of being consumed by the Divine. This is an apt description, for ritual is indeed a kind of consummation in which, as in a sexual union, the result is completion: two halves becoming fused as one. Those who experience the first sensations of transformation within ritual are often overwhelmed at the feelings that erupt within them. Sometimes a feeling of mergence and oneness arises immediately. At other times, it comes on slowly. One may go through the motions of ritual for a long time with little to no sensation at all as the logical mind muddles over the process of figuring out the rhythm and sequence of the movements. Eventually, however, one learns to dance with the cosmos without thought, until reaching a state where there is no dancer, no cosmos—only the dance. Or as in making love, when one reaches that sublime state where the body takes over and the mind lets go, and suddenly there are no lovers, only the energy that flows between them. It is by accessing this place in ritual—as in dance or in lovemaking—that the heart opens to the power of Spirit and union occurs.

One evening I was leading a ritual that I had done only once or twice before. I was feeling self-conscious about my role and found myself hyper-aware of making sure that I was doing all the steps correctly. The ritual was about halfway through when I reached a place where all thought vanished and I was sucked into the rhythm of the process. My body felt as though it was moving without my conscious guidance. At that moment, I lost all orientation to my place in the room, which now felt very small around me, and I very big within it. I felt a surge of energy run through me, as if I had just disconnected from my body and "plugged in" to some great energy source. The momentum carried me to the end of the ritual and left me full. Later, when I described the experience to my teacher, he said, "That flash of something bigger than yourself is power itself, letting you know it has descended upon you. Isn't it the best?"

As with dancing or making love, when we finally surrender to the experience and allow ourselves to connect with something outside of ourselves—which is, in fact, our greater selves—one has reached the state of illumination and mergence. In this place, time and space are abolished as the sacred and the profane interpenetrate. The shaman steps out of the boundaries of ordinary time and space into what has been called alternately "sacred time," "mythic time," "primordial time," "all-time," and even "no time." In *The Sacred and the Profane*, Eliade explains it as time that is "always the same, which belongs to eternity"[12] and "the eternal presence of the mystical event."[13] This is where magic takes place.

Says Albert Villoldo, teacher of Inca shamanism and author of *Dance of the Four Winds*:

> There are two kinds of time. In the West we recognize only the kind of time that flies like an arrow, which is linear time. The problem with linear time is that the main operating principle within it is causality: cause and effect. The problem with causality is that it says that who you are today is a result of an earlier cause of something that happened yesterday or the day before yesterday or ten years ago or twenty years ago. In linear time, the present is always claimed by the past. In the medicine tradition, there is another kind of time, called "sacred time"—time that turns like a wheel.... The beauty of stepping outside of linear time and into sacred time is that sacred time is noncausal. In sacred time, you can influence events that happened in the past. It is also where you can nudge destiny.... When you step outside of linear time into sacred time, you can break free of the momentum of linear time and choose your destiny.[14]

Ritual provides a space where individuals, guided by the expertise of the shaman, can pass safely out of linear time, time that is stuck in a continuous cycle of cause and effect. By drawing oneself past the limiting temporal existence of linear time and into this "succession of eternities," it becomes possible for the shaman and ritual participants to cause dramatic changes to occur in the physical realm.

"The chaos theory postulates that a tropical storm in the Caribbean can be started by a butterfly flapping its wings in Beijing," explains Villoldo. "The tropical storm exists in ordinary time and is very difficult to change. But, in sacred time, you can avert it while it is still whisper of wind on the edge of a butterfly's wings. All you would need to do is blow on it."

Because sacred space and time are free from the cycle of cause and effect that distinguish linear time, working within this context allows for seemingly miraculous events to occur within the physical plane. This may cause one to ask, if this is true, why isn't everyone running around changing the world to suit our desires? Most likely *we are*, at least to some extent—though perhaps our brains lack the capacity to see the cause and effect of our thoughts upon the world. In terms of ritual, what is also likely is that the reason the majority of us cannot create similarly dramatic transformations as the shaman is that we lack the proper focus and ability to get ourselves out of the rut of the "literal," consensual world. As Margot Adler wrote in *Drawing Down the Moon*, "Those who do magic are those who work with techniques that alter consciousness in order to facilitate psychic activity."[15]

Here is where a distinction can be made between magic, a kind of ecstatic prayer, and the more passive form of prayer found in some religions. Although all forms of prayer have their own consciousness-altering properties, ecstatic prayer has been called "not just a meditation about God, but a 'going out of oneself' toward God."[16] The infamous magician Aleister Crowley defined magic as "the art and science of causing changes to occur in conformity with the will."[17] When ecstatic prayer and mergence are combined with human will, the result is a dramatic transformation in the physical world.

Of course, tapping into the power of being able to effect change in the physical world through spiritual means is something that has great potential for misuse and therefore carries with it great responsibility. As many have discovered, forcing one's will over the rhythm of the cosmos can have disastrous results.

"When supernatural events occur through mortal intervention, it is sorcery," writes Gershon Winkler in *Magic of the Ordinary*. "Bad sorcery involves the misuse of supernal powers to take advantage of people and to intimidate them; good sorcery involves the channeling of supernal powers to heal, to uplift, and to do so with the awareness that the Creator is the ultimate source of all those feats and of whether they are effective or not."[18]

Through the ritual process, the shaman steps out of an ego state that can cloud the distinction between "good" and "bad" sorcery. By doing so, he or she finds the balance between the passive request of "*thy* will be done" and the more active intent of "*My* will be done." Here, the shaman achieves a state of ecstasy in which divine will and human will are united, where the flow of the natural order merges with personal intention.

There is a famous story told by Carl Jung, attributed to Richard Wilhelm, translator of the *I Ching*, about a rainmaker who was asked to come make rain for a village that was experiencing a long and devastating drought. Though others had tried, no other holy man had been successful, and the village was on the edge of starvation. The first thing the rainmaker did was ask to be given a hut, into which he secluded himself for four days and four nights until it began to snow.

Of course, Wilhelm wanted to know how he had done this. The rainmaker told him that when he came into the village he had noticed that the villagers were out of harmony with Heaven and Earth. As soon as the rainmaker brought *himself* into harmony with Heaven and Earth, the snow came.

Compare this solution to that of how we in the modern world have been taught to resolve such a problem. The response more likely would be to announce a state of emergency, get federal funding, and call in the best engineer to make a plan to reroute a dam—in other words, to try to "fix" it in some concrete, tangible way. Imagine the response if that engineer, as Wilhelm's rainmaker did, decided to just sit and align himself with the cosmos! Such non-doing would be meaningless, even considered negligent, to a culture raised to actively "do" and "fix." That engineer would most likely be fired on the spot.

Although there is nothing wrong with active doing, per se, one cannot overlook the dramatic transformations that can occur through creating this magical resonance with the spirit world. We can see it in the myriad stories of a shaman curing someone of a life-threatening disease with no more than a few chants and motions.

This is an extreme example, and transformation can also take place on a subtler, more personal level. It has been well established that ritual can have a profound effect on the emotional well-being of an individual. In the same way that ritual is a reenactment of myth on a cosmic level, ritual also reflects an individual's life myth. Where the individual places him or herself in the ritual space can be seen as representing his or her place within a personal stage of evolution. Ritual allows one to orient oneself within the cosmos and place oneself in a larger context. Because of this, transformation can take place.

During this phase of the ritual process, participants may be invited to make some sort of symbolic sacrifice to the fire or whatever the focal point of the ceremony happens to be. Often this offering will represent something that the individual desires to draw into his or her life or something that he or she wishes to release. The psyche cannot differentiate between an actual act and a symbolic one, and any physical event will be registered at the deepest levels of the psyche. In the context of ritual, these symbolic transformations become actual ones. If someone in a ritual releases the symbol of, say, an addiction, at some level the psyche fully believes the transformation has occurred. In *Inner Work*, Robert Johnson tells the story of the famous Jungian analyst Toni Wolffe, who insisted that her patients turn their inner process, especially their dreams, into an actual physical action:

> She met her patients at the door, and before they could even get into a chair, she would demand: "And what did you do about that dream from last week?" Patients who had done something specific, something concrete and physical, were safe from the wrath to come. But if they hemmed and hawed, said they had thought about it a little, had talked with someone about it, or some such vague thing, she would turn them around and steer them back through the door. As the door was slamming behind them, she would say: "Come back when you mean business."[19]

According to Johnson, Wolffe would say, "People can analyze for twenty years, and nothing below the neck is aware that anything is going on! You have to do something about it. Do something with your muscles!"[20]

> The role of ritual in the growth of consciousness is related to its power to make symbolic experience into something physical and concrete.... Although we can understand the meaning of symbols with our minds, our understanding is made immeasurably deeper and more concrete when we *feel* the symbols with our bodies and our feelings. When we only think about symbols, or talk about them, we are able to detach ourselves too readily from the feeling quality that surrounds them. But if we *do* something to express the symbol—something that involves our bodies and our emotions—the symbol becomes a living reality for us. It etches itself indelibly on our consciousness.[21]

Through acts of worship, such as ritual, a connection is established, completing the circuit between spiritual and physical, inner and outer, so that transformations can be made.

Return to the Profane

The ritual comes to a close with the shaman and participants thanking the spirit allies, the four directions, Heaven, and Earth for their assistance and participation in the ceremony. Once the ceremonial space has been closed, various arrangements are made for dismantling the ceremonial structure (or not dismantling it, whichever the case may be). Participants are gently transitioned out of sacred space, back to the world of the profane, often with food, drink, and any other grounding agents to help reestablish them in the physical world.

The shaman may prescribe daily practices to keep the intent of the ritual strong even after the ritual is over. I once did a ritual for a friend of mine who was getting married. In the ritual, I had her symbolically release any fears and hindering thought patterns that were keeping her from going into this union fully. Once the ritual was over, I told her that, although her symbolic actions had removed that thought pattern from her, for the next few days she might feel the presence of those old fears circling closely around her as "hungry ghosts."[22] I recommended that she not allow herself to let these thoughts back in or the same fears would be with her again. She hesitated at this and admitted that, as much as she wanted to be rid of it, a part of her had a hard time letting go of her fear. This is not unusual, as most of us feel dependent upon our fears and shadows. As much as we think we want to be rid of them, a part of us believes that they are the only things that keep us safe and functioning in the world. Therefore, letting go of them can leave one feeling exposed and vulnerable. After my friend said this, I suggested that she then think of it just as a two-week break. For those two weeks she was to give herself permission not to allow the hungry ghosts back into her consciousness. After those two weeks were up, I told her, she was free to invite them back into her again if she chose.

She liked this idea, because it took some of the pressure off. As long as she knew that this was only temporary, that she would not be left exposed and open this way forever, she was able to think about it without being overwhelmed. In this way it is a lot like the Twelve-Step slogan of "one day at a time." On her own impulse, throughout those next two weeks she left offerings of food outside her door for the hungry ghosts to feed upon so that they would not be constantly looking to her for nourishment. As the days went on, her own personal power system began to fill the spaces that the ghosts had left. By the end of two weeks, as their presence began to fade, she no longer felt as though she needed to invite those fears back in order to be whole and safe.

Reconnecting to the Unseen

It is no coincidence that the process of ritual has found a place in the practices of every religious and spiritual tradition known to humankind. Reconnecting to the Divine is a vital element to the health of the individual and community. For me, the ritual process has been the greatest tool I have found for creating emotional, spiritual, and physical change within my own life. The infrequency of this kind of ecstatic and in-tentional ritual in our modern world means a great loss to our collective soul. The loss of connection to something that exists outside of our "little selves" leaves us hungry for an experience of the sacred. Without the opportunity to consciously dia-logue with our allies in the spirit realm, from whom we may ask for help and guidance, we spend our lives trying to "tough it out" on our own, instead of utilizing a great source of strength and support that exists in those invisible realms. Reconnect-ing to the sacred through ritual enables us to release the bur-den of control over our daily lives, allowing us to let go and float effortlessly within the liquid sea of the universe.

Exercises

Exercise #13: Creating Sacred Space

Create a sacred space for yourself to do your work. The space can be indoors or outdoors. You can design an entire room this way, or you can create an altar small enough to fit on a side table, or anything in between. Make this space a reflection of the cosmos within you and outside of you. Make sure you have the four directions and their elements represented (such as a shell in the West symbolizing water), the Upper, Middle, and Lower Worlds (here add the representations of your spirit allies that you gathered in the last exercise), and the center pillar. As you create this space, look back in your journal to see what your experiences were as you were attuning to the four directions, three worlds, and the center pillar. Add any items that are sacred to you, that help you feel connected to spirit. Have fun with this. Make it meaningful to you. Beauty is a power and a blessing and is nourishing to the unseen world. Making your altar beautiful reaches that place of awe and reverence within you. It calls to your senses and to your spirit as well as those allies that you have chosen to honor with this act of reverence. Put a representation of your shadow in here as well. Treat it kindly and respectfully, as it is part of you and a source of power when used correctly. Don't be concerned about what other people have done. This is your universe to create as you like. Just as you are a microcosm of the universe, the altar is a microcosm of you (and therefore the universe as well!).

I spent years working with an altar that I felt very little connection to—or, rather, *trying* to work with it. I was being a very dutiful student. The items and their placement reflected what my teachers had taught me, as well as what I had seen from other students in this work. And still, no matter how hard I tried, I never felt fully connected to my altar or most of the items on it. Then one day, out of pure frustration, I completely dismantled it (blessing and thanking each of the objects as I "retired" them) and began again. This time I disregarded everything I had been taught to include and only put things on it that truly made that spark of reverence and beauty ignite inside me. I went through my house and found the items that were most meaningful, most magical to me: a statue, a piece of fabric, a book. Just doing this—figuring out what was most significant and beautiful in my life—was an amazing process of self-discovery. Once I was done, I found I had an even better understanding of the person that I am and, along with that, a tremendous sense of self-empowerment. My altar became something not so much created but discovered, much in the same way that Michelangelo said that he did not create a statue from the stone, but rather uncovered it from within the layers under which it was hiding.

Once you have "discovered" your altar, create a daily ritual for attuning to it. Follow the stages outlined in this chapter as you do so: creation of sacred space, purification, invocation, mergence (in which you might try going into a journeying state), and, finally, worldly return. Be aware that an altar becomes its own entity and, therefore, must be cared for regularly. Just as a houseplant needs regular watering, an altar must similarly be "fed." The food that the altar feeds upon is prayer, intent, and gratitude. It can be thought of as having a child: Once you bring it to life, it is negligent not to keep feeding it. When you are done, thank your guides and spirits that you have called in and tell them that they may leave now if they so choose. Record your experiences.

Chapter 6

In Praise of the Rainmaker: Shamanic Healing

Ipupiara Makunaiman was born into the *Ureu-eu-wau-wau*, a remote Brazilian tribe whose name translates into "people from the stars." According to legend, the Ureu-eu-wau-wau people originally came from a planet near the Pleiades. A prophet among them predicted that the inhabitants of a distant planet named Earth were doomed, destined to consume themselves into extinction. As the story goes, the emissaries traveled to Earth, to the jungles of the Amazon, where they would await the time when they would spread their knowledge. Ipupiara, whose name means "freshwater dolphin," is one of the last few members of what was once a well-populated tribe.

As a young man, Ipupiara was influenced greatly by the ways of the tribal community in which he lived. His Ureu-eu-wau-wau mother had always told him that she saw a future for him as a shaman and predicted that one day he would be a leader in his community. His Portuguese merchant father had different ideas and sent Ipupiara off to the university with the hope that his son might become a medical doctor. At the university, Ipupiara began to feel ashamed of his native roots. In a conversation one day, he told me:

> I wouldn't dare to tell the girls that I have indigenous blood in my veins. I didn't want my mother to come to the university because she had the shape and the face of indigenous woman. But the Great Spirit works in very mysterious ways. When I was almost finished at the university, I got sick. Really sick. My father took me to the doctor, but they couldn't find what I had. They made a lot of tests and nothing was wrong with me. But that wasn't possible. I was sick. I was losing energy. I was having pain. My father kept sending me to different doctors, but they never could find what I had.
>
> Finally, my mother said "You are sick, son. The doctors can't find what you have. You have to go to our village. The shaman will fix you." I said, "No, mom. If the white doctors can't, the shaman will never fix me." I got worse. I was incapable of moving. I lay in the bed. I knew I was dying. It came to the point that I barely could pronounce words. The family doctor told my mother and my father that I wouldn't survive. My mother said to me again, "Son, you are really sick. You are dying. There's nothing that the doctors can do, but give me a chance to take you to the village to be healed by the shaman." When she told me that I was scared, so I agreed. They took me to the village. I was feeling weaker and weaker. I felt my soul departing. When I saw the shaman dancing and chanting around me I thought, "Ipu, you are done for." I thought he was going to kill me. I remember that the old man came with a bowl of greenish stuff. They knew that I was incapable of drinking, so they open[ed] my mouth and poured the stuff down my mouth. It was bitter.

Really, really bitter. When it hit my stomach, it felt like a hot pepper burning the inside of me. I felt warmth going through my body. Then I fell asleep. I slept the whole night through. The next morning, I asked them to help me sit up and I told my mother I was hungry. In one week I was walking and talking. It was then I realized that my mom was right. There is something far beyond our comprehension that can help us. Because of it, I am here now.[1]

When he had fully recovered, Ipupiara began an apprenticeship to learn the medicine ways of his people. His mother's prediction came true, and he was eventually initiated as a shaman in the Ureu-eu-wau-wau tradition.

The Roots of Illness

Unlike western medicine, with its seemingly infinite number of causes and cures for disease, in shamanic philosophy all illness—emotional, mental, and physical—is viewed as being the result of some spiritual manifestation beyond physical reality. When someone is sick, it is believed that the person must first address the spiritual element causing the illness before any kind of lasting healing can be achieved. This is where the shaman fulfills a vital role in his or her community, for issues of the spirit are undeniably the domain of the shaman. With his or her experience communicating with the spirit world, only the shaman can accurately diagnose the spiritual roots of an illness and communicate with the spirit world in order to restore balance.

As it is for many initiates, Ipupiara's calling to the path came in the form of what has been called a "shamanic illness," some physical or mental illness that forces the neophyte to become his or her own first patient. The shaman's initiatory healing crisis therefore becomes one of self-transformation in which the "wounded healer" must first turn inward to heal the self. As in the story of the rainmaker, the shaman must first bring him or herself into balance and harmony with the cosmos before being able to effect change. In fact, in some shamanic traditions, the shaman is said to actually transfer the sickness from the client to him or herself, then do battle against the evil spirits or negative energies that now exist within the shaman.[2] Another way of looking at this is that the shaman merges into oneness with his client, and therefore the client's illness and imbalance suddenly becomes the shaman's as well. Here we can understand one of the perils of undertaking the shamanic path. The shaman, as healer, must become a "warrior," constantly doing battle against the negative forces that cause disease, even perhaps intentionally bringing these influences within himself, each time he or she undertakes a client for healing.

Just as an unhealthy state is seen as the result of negative influences, health can likewise only occur when the client is in harmony with the sacred. Most illness, therefore, is seen as the result of a breakage in the relationship with the spirit world. This breakage can occur when a person's connection to his or her spirit allies is loosened or severed, either by his or her own actions (such as violating certain taboos or spiritual laws) or by ill-intended people or spirits that are trying to do the person harm. When this essential relationship is out of balance or the connection broken, the individual (or community, planet, or any such system) experiences a loss of personal power that creates a deficiency (similar to a weakened immune system) that allows illness and psycho-spiritual disturbances to take hold. The shaman's healing rituals are aimed in large part at counteracting this threat by reestablishing the vital link between the client and his or her spirit allies. All healings, therefore, involve some form of restoration of power, life force, or soul, as well as the removal of harmful energies that have filled a weakness created by the loss of these "mystical organs."

Diagnosis

Once called upon to treat a client, the shaman's first step is to determine the exact nature of the illness as well as the course of action to be taken in order to restore balance to the client.

Diagnosis can take many forms. The way in which illness appears in the physical may provide clues as to the spiritual nature of the ailment. For example, if the patient's illness is due to a loss of personal power, such as soul loss, it may manifest as psychological disturbances such as chronic depression and/or the feeling of being fragmented or "not all there." Chronic illnesses are often attributed to soul loss. The most extreme example of this is a coma, which is viewed as a total— as opposed to partial—soul loss.[3] In the case of spiritual intrusions or other energy blockages, the patient will often suffer a localized pain rather than chronic pain or mental disturbances.[4] An intrusion is often found at the site of malignancies, such as cancer, or certain emotional pain, such as heartbreak.[5]

However, according to shamanic diagnostic practices, simply viewing the outwardly manifested physical and mental symptoms never leads to a one-size-fits-all solution. Unlike modern medicine, shamanism does not focus on the illness within the person, but rather the person holding the illness. Although the shaman may prescribe herbs to treat a malady as a medical doctor might prescribe a pill, the shaman's diagnostic decision does not come from matching up symptoms to a cure but by consulting with his or her spirit allies about each individual case.

Besides going into ecstatic trance in order to determine the nature of illness and its treatments, the shaman may also rely on any number of divinatory tools and extrasensory techniques to get in touch with his or her allies. This may include reading signs or omens in nature, as well as consulting the patterns revealed by "randomly" placed objects such as cards, animal entrails, shells, stones, or leaves, just to name a few. In some cases, the way in which the objects place themselves in relation to the shaman is significant. For example, the number of leaves or shells facing upwards may have one meaning, whereas a different number or arrangement may signify something else. The shaman may also use the spontaneous patterns as a vehicle for bringing symbolic messages from the depths of the unconscious mind. In Siberia, Ulchi shamans determine the cause of illness by consulting a *ponga saiven*, a carved statue attached to a leather strap, which is used much in the same way as a pendulum is in the west.[6] In some South American traditions, a shaman may diagnose the client's condition by rubbing either an egg or live guinea pig over the patient's body, believing that the illness will then be mirrored by the innards of the animal or egg. The egg is cracked open or the guinea pig dissected and an assessment of the patient's conditions made.

Spiritual Intrusions

Through diagnosis, the shaman may determine that the patient's illness is the result of a spiritual intrusion or blockage that has become lodged within the patient's body. These "magical objects" are said to be invisibly projected into the body by sorcerers or evil spirits using negative thought forms. Says Eliade in *Shamanism*, "The magician does not introduce them *in concreto* but creates them by power of thought."[7] A spiritual intrusion or blockage may also turn out to be possession by an evil spirit. Although the form that these intrusions may take is limitless, most intrusions manifest as objects that would be considered repulsive to the shaman or client, such as worms, nails, putrid meat, and any other unpleasant items that are believed to be the cause of the patient's discomfort and degeneration. The removal of such objects can be fierce, as the shaman's treatments can involve removal of the offending spirit or objects by beating, biting, or sucking on the patient. Other times, the shaman may use a variety of techniques to frighten or trick an evil spirit out of the body. After successfully removing the intrusion, the shaman will often capture or blow it into a fetish or into the fire to be transformed.

Whether these intrusions are to be viewed as actual physical objects or as symbolic representations of illness is up for debate. Some shamans insist that their experiences are indeed ones of extracting physical, tangible objects from their patients' bodies. Brant Secunda explained to me:

> The Huichols heal by going into a mild trance, during which they travel into the Nierica—the doorway that connects our heart to all of Creation. There, the shaman would talk to the deer spirit and ask for guidance as to what to do for the person. The shaman then might brush grass or a feather, or something like that, over the patient. This acts like a x-ray machine so that the shaman can look inside the body. Ideally, the patient should look clear, like a crystal. Where the energy is not clear—where there is darkness—is where the illness is. Once the location of the illness is identified, the shaman will send the spirit of the deer inside the patient....
>
> Once the deer spirit has done the healing, the shaman will suck the illness out of the patient's body. Often the sickness will come out of the body in the form of a stone or a bone or a worm or blood—something that would defy our model of reality. The shaman will spit that out and immediately give it to the Earth or to the fire to be purified.[8]

Others describe these intrusions more as symbolic representations of the illness than tangible objects. Sandra Ingerman, author of *Soul Retrieval*, describes these symbols as manifestations of the disease's "spiritual identity." She says:

> All illness has a spiritual identity. This means that when I journey into a client's body to look at illness, it will

actually have an identity. It will look like fanged reptile, or an insect, or some dark, sludgy material. The illness will show itself in a form that is repulsive to me. Some of the modern work being done with imagery and healing correlates with what shamans have always seen with illness. For example, when patients with cancer draw what their illness looks like, they often draw fanged reptiles and insects. People see on their own what classical shamans have always seen.[9]

This distinction between intrusions that are "real" and those that are "representational" is less important than one might initially think. As we've seen in past chapters, symbolic action has an immensely powerful effect upon the psyche, which is why ritual and the ritual process can be used to achieve remarkable results in the physical, mental, emotional, and spiritual health of an individual. Even as symbolic representations, an intrusion holds just as much power over the patient's health as any tangible, physical object.

This technique of using symbolic action to create health in an individual is where western psychology and shamanism both meet and diverge. As shamanism does, many western psychological practices use symbolic imagery to effect change in the consciousness of an individual. However, it is important to note that, although shamanism and psychology both work on the symbolic level, the way the symbols are viewed and utilized differ significantly. For example, say there is an individual who is unable to sleep due to recurring nightmares about being stung repeatedly by bees. In order to relieve the person of the nightmare, a western psychological approach would be to view the bees as a symbolic representation of an emotional problem. The psychologist would therefore work with the client to uncover the symbol's underlying meaning. If the therapist and client determined that the bees were representations of feelings of powerlessness in the client's life, the two together might then work on reconciling that emotional pattern.

According to this approach, once the client's feelings of powerless are reconciled, the nightmare would cease to happen.

The shaman, on the other hand, is more likely to see the bees themselves as the cause of the patient's feelings of powerlessness, and not the other way around. In other words, instead of seeing the bees as important only in terms of their greater underlying meaning, the shaman sees the symbol itself as the problem and the resulting anxiety (such as feelings of powerlessness) as the *byproduct* of the symbol, not its *cause*. Because of this, in the shamanic way of working, removal of the symbol and its energetic imprint from the psyche through ritual is required. Many shamans say that they consider this method of working to be superior to the western psychological method, which they see as unnecessarily slow in its treatment. Whereas western psychology may take years to uncover, come to terms with, and remove the thought pattern or neurosis from the psyche, through this model, a healthy emotional or physical state can be achieved instantaneously through the energetic extraction of the intruding symbol within the psyche.

Restoration of Personal Power

As we have seen, whether or not an intrusion is tangible or symbolic does not make a difference. The psyche, which does not make such distinctions as "real" or "unreal" except where the belief systems and ideas of the ego mind create conflict, will react in a similar manner either way. Just as the shaman can restore health to the patient by increasing personal power, a sorcerer may likewise harm an individual using these same methods. In the end, the only difference between the techniques used to harm and those used to heal is the intent behind them. Most of us have heard of the idea that the sorcerer's curses work by the sorcerer implanting a negative symbol into a victim. This negativity eats away at the victim's psyche, causing the physical or emotional trauma. Knowing what we now know about the power of the mind over the state of the body, it does not seem far-fetched that words or symbols have a great power in transforming an individual's state of health, both for better and for worse. When a doctor tells a patient that he or she has three months to live, that is, in effect, a kind of curse that can effect the patient's reality.

In order to test this idea, I once asked a shaman to cut my "luminous threads," in order to create an energetic disturbance in my body. At the time, I didn't really believe that anything he did would affect me, that something like that could be done by will alone. Although he was reluctant at first, after I badgered him into it, the shaman eventually agreed to do so. He performed a series of gestures in front of me. At first, nothing seemed to happen. The next thing I knew, I was doubled over on the ground, shaking, with an intense nausea spreading over me. Although the shaman restored my power soon after, it took several hours for the nausea to subside. I was profoundly humbled.

Despite my conscious skepticism before the fact, I do not discount the possibility that my sudden illness could have been caused by the power of suggestion. Perhaps I had brought the attack upon myself by some deep, unconscious part of me that really *did* believe in the shaman's power. Then again, perhaps he *had* created that effect by his intent alone. Or, more likely, it was *both*. The point I make here, however, is that, in the end, it doesn't matter *how* it happened, but rather that it *did* happen. Again, psychology does not negate magic; it is simply one element of the process that makes it work.

It is not, however, the whole process. What may be harder to grasp for all of us is the way any kind of manipulation, whether harming or healing, works when the individual is not consciously aware of it. However, even science has proven that it does work in a very real and tangible way. Studies have shown that a patient's chances for survival rise dramatically when that person is prayed for—even if he or she is unaware that it is being done. In shamanism's holographic view of the world, time and space are not obstacles. Our unconscious selves are, at all times, recording all actions taking place within the cosmos. A sorcerer's negative actions upon, say, a voodoo doll or similar symbolic representation of the intended victim are merely the microcosm of the macrocosm. Any effect on the one will ripple out in energetic waves, creating unconscious disturbances in the other.

Soul Loss

A loss of personal power is believed by the majority of shamanic traditions around the world to be with a result of one root cause: soul loss. That is, the loss of parts of the individual's vital essence or life force. Unlike some religious traditions that believe in a single, unified soul, indigenous people more often than not hold the belief that each person contains multiple soul parts, each of which engages in various functions to keep the individual whole and healthy. According to the Ulchi people, human beings have three souls each: one housed in the heart, one that travels in dreams at night, and one similar to the concept of the astral body that is prone to wandering or being captured by evil spirits.[10]

Soul loss can occur for different reasons. In some cases, the soul may choose to depart on its own. This often occurs during times of trauma, in which a piece of the soul leaves in order to survive emotional or physical pain. In psychological terms, this is referred to as "dissociation." In a similar way that shamans view soul loss, psychologists recognize dissociation as part of the psyche's self-protection mechanism, leading to disturbances in the integration of identity, memory, or consciousness.

Certain soul parts are also said to be vulnerable to theft by malevolent spirits or by sorcerers who, for whatever reason, may wish to diminish the power of an individual, thus causing illness or death. Soul stealing, says Sandra Ingerman, can also happened unintentionally—even in places where the idea of soul stealing is not a part of the collective paradigm:

> In many shamanic cultures, soul stealing is done on a very conscious level, as a form of psychic warfare. The East Indian term for soul stealing is "psychic vampirism," because when you steal somebody's soul, you attempt to take some of their energy.

> In this culture, pretty much all of us steal souls, but we are not aware of what we are doing. Perhaps we are attracted to somebody's energy. It looks like this person has a lot more power than we do, and we think that if we could just have some of that, our lives would be better. So we take a piece of their soul. The difference is that here most of us steal souls out of ignorance. If you said to someone, "Do you realize that you are stealing that soul?" they would look at you like you were crazy.[11]

When one of these soul parts wanders away, gets lost, or is stolen by a sorcerer or evil spirit, the individual is no longer his or her whole self and therefore can easily become diminished, physically, mentally, and spiritually. Without one or more of these essential parts, the individual is left unstable and open to intrusion. As a way of counteracting this negative energy, the shaman in his or her healings will work on increasing the individual's personal power to a point where there is no weakness or void to be exploited by these energies. The shaman's job therefore includes traveling into non-ordinary reality in order to track down the missing or stolen soul part and return it to the client. This can be difficult, sometimes even downright dangerous, as the soul may be reluctant to return to a place that it believes to be unsafe. In the case of soul theft, the shaman may need to do battle with malignant forces in order to wrestle the spirit away and bring it back to the body of the client.

According to Eliade, in the healing rituals of the Dyaks of Borneo, once an illness is determined to be caused by an evil spirit, a ceremony is enacted to expel the spirit from the client using special tools. She writes:

> The Sea Dyak shaman is called *manang*.... The *manang* has a box containing a quantity of magical objects, the most important of which are quartz crystals, *bata ilau* ("the stones of light"), by help of which the shaman discovers the patient's soul. For, here too, illness is a flight of the soul and the purpose of the séance is to discover it and restore it to its place in the body. The seance takes place at night. The patient's body is rubbed with stones, then the audience begins to intone monotonous songs while the chief *manang* dances to the point of exhaustion; it is thus that he seeks and summons the patient's soul. If the illness is serious, the soul escapes from the *manang*'s hands several times. Once the leading shaman falls to the ground, a blanket is thrown over him, and the audience awaits the result of his ecstatic journey. For as soon as he is in ecstasy the *manang* goes down to the underworld in search of the patient's soul. Finally he captures it, and suddenly rises, holding it in his hand, then replaces it through the skull.[12]

In order to track down and retrieve the missing soul part, then, the shaman's consciousness must merge into oneness with the client, traveling into the client's unconscious depths in which the missing soul may be hiding. In the 2000 film, *The Cell*, Jennifer Lopez has, with the help of technology, the ability to travel into the minds of coma victims. Within their psyches, she discovers surreal landscapes in which are hidden memories of events that are responsible for this "loss of soul." Likewise, the shaman enters into resonance with the client, enters into non-ordinary reality, and, with the help of his or her spirit allies, reclaims the missing parts that are responsible for the patient's loss of personal power.

After my own soul retrieval, I felt so filled with energy that I did not sleep for two days.

Rituals of Healing

Healing is often a two-part process that may first include a removal of unwanted energies and intrusions, followed by the restoration of the individual's soul, personal power, or vital life force. When the energy channels of the body are cleared from blockages, personal power is, as a result, able to be restored. Rabbi Gershon Winkler described this healing process to me in detail:

> In our tradition, we believe that most diseases are a "plumbing problem," meaning that our health is dependent upon how open the channels of our body are. What the shaman does is conduct a ceremony to open up the channels and find out what part of the person is being clogged or is out of balance. The ceremony includes eight phases of movement to shake the blockage loose.[13]

The healing begins with the establishment of sacred space. According to Winkler:

> To prepare the space for the healing, the first thing you do is take a stick and draw on the earth the six-pointed star called *magen*, or "the shield." This symbol is also known as the Star of David. It symbolizes the four winds, sky and earth. The *magen* is designed to guard both the healer and the patient against the *Sit'ra Ach'ra*.

> The first of the eight movements of the healing is called *s'michah*, which means "leaning." As the healer, you would face north and lean with all your weight on the person long enough to meditate your presence into harmony with theirs, so that their buffer zone is relaxed and welcoming to you.

When that is done, you put a stone in each of the patient's hands—one heavier than the other. Which hand gets which stone depends on what part of the patient needs balancing. The right side is symbolic of the universe's desire to swallow. It manifests in a feeling of lack of control. The left side represents the stepping back, allowing for a piecing together.

The second movement is called *ta'nufah*, or "swaying." Here, you face the east, gently grab the person and move them back and forth in a circular motion in order to shake loose the energy that you want to work with.

The third movement is called *hagashah*, or "bringing near." Facing west, you now escort the patient into sacred space; into the center of the shield. At this point, you would face the person in the direction that addresses whatever kind of healing they need. If they have a block in their ability to start something new in life, you would face them to the east, the place of beginning. If they have an issue regarding self-image, you would face them to the south, the place of cleansing. If it's a problem with a relationship—which necessitates blending and merging—or with facing death, which is also has to do with blending and merging—you face them to the west. If they have a problem with mystery—say they have just came out of a seminar and are totally boggled—you face them to the north, the place of mystery.

The fourth movement is called *k'mitzah*, "grabbing." Here you would face south and move your hands in an upwards motion around their field without touching them, grabbing their energy—the *diyuk'na*. *Diyuk'na* is the Aramaic word for the astral body. You grab the astral body and seize the energy that is around the person, starting from the earth and moving up. Then you grab a handful of earth or flour or anything that is of the earth that has not been processed, and sprinkle all over the person. This is done as a way of bringing the energy of the earth to the patient.

The fifth movement is *haza'ah*, "sprinkling." This time it is done with water or, preferably, flower and plant oils. You take some on your index finger of both hands, and thrust the index fingers at them. You don't direct where it lands, because, at that point, it's not in your hands anymore. It just lands where it is supposed to land.

The sixth is *hak'tarah*, "smoking." Here, you smudge the patient with leaves that you have gathered. You also light a three-wicked candle and, as the smoke is rising, you move the fire back and forth in front of their eyes, which are closed. This brings the spirit aspect of the self to the forefront, so that it can connect with the smoke—the smoke representing the return of matter to spirit. The three wicks of the flame represent the three ways in which the soul manifests in the person: physically, emotionally, and intellectually.

At this point you take a ram's horn, called a *shofar*, and have the patient blow their breath into the wider opening of the horn. You then cup your hand over it and blow the sound of the horn in a bunch of short successive notes. When used properly, the *shofar* has the power to shatter the physical, spiritual, and emotional constitution of the person so that the healer can then realign the patient where they have been out of balance.

The seventh movement is called *m'likah*, "squeezing." You embrace the person tightly and squeeze out the negativity or the obstruction that is causing their sickness. You cradle them in your intention to heal them. After you release them from the squeezing, you take the rocks from each of their hands and throw them in opposite directions from one another in order to split up the absorbed negativity. Each stone needs a separate space to do its transformative work. If they land near one another, it invites confusion into the patient.

The eighth and final phase is called *hak'balah*, "receiving." If there are friends around, when you release them from the embrace, you let them drop into their friends. If there is no one else there, then you allow the person to drop into the elements, such as onto the earth or against a tree.

The person that does the healing then needs to walk away and not come back so that the patient isn't distracted by your presence, thereby stepping out of the moment and the experience. It is also important to do this so that the power behind the healing is not attributed to you.[14]

You cannot change a situation with the same consciousness that created it. As we explored in the last chapter, through the ritual process a connection is established in which the shaman guides his or her client into resonance with the spirit world. A new mode of consciousness is established for the patient, creating an ideal mental, emotional, physical, and spiritual state for healing to take place.

Shaman as the Tools of Spirit

Winkler's final statement is an important one. Just about all the shamans I've talked to are quick to say that they themselves are not responsible for the healing. The real power to heal and transform, they say, comes from the spirit world itself. Ipupiara agreed, telling me:

That is the crucial part. When a shaman is working, he or she is just a vessel. Recently I had a woman come to me who had cancer. I asked her "Why did you come here to see me?" She said, "Oh, because I learned from other people that you are powerful." I told her, "I am not powerful. Mother Earth is the one that is powerful. I am just the switch that will connect you with Mother Earth." I am not the one doing the healing. You are not the one doing the healing. It is Mother Earth doing the healing. That is why, as a healer, you have to learn how to interact with the spirits. As soon as you know how to interact with spirits, it is easy for you to do healings. If I know that you are coming for a healing, I will call upon the spirit that protects me, helps me, the one that resides inside of me. I will ask them to be around me and to guide me, because I'll be just a channel. That's the reason why some traditions use hallucinogenic substances. They use hallucinogenic stuff to get disconnected from this realm. If you can block yourself to this realm here, then you can fully connect to that dimension and to the spirits. This is the best way to do a healing. The moment you get disconnected, things work. If you allow the spirits to work through you, you can do things that will surprise you. When a person gets into this work they begin to see amazing things happen—things that from a Western world perspective are too much to be true and too much to believe. But if you really change your way of thinking and just allow yourself to be a tool in Mother Earth's hands, you can do miracles.[15]

Brant Secunda echoes this sentiment as well:

The Huichols say that nothing is impossible for the gods to heal. Don José once healed a man who had slashed his Achilles tendon with a machete. Normally, the man would never walk again, but within a month after the healing he was back walking out in his cornfield with only a very slight limp. I met my wife when she came to me for a healing. She had a fatal form of hepatitis and couldn't eat. She weighed about seventy-seven pounds. After the healing, she gained thirty pounds in two weeks. Then there was another case that I worked on that is the only documented case of pancreatic cancer reversing itself.[16]

But, then, if all things can be healed by spirit, do we need western medicine at all? Ipupiara answered me this way:

> We do need medicine. But, you know, our mind is the most powerful medicine of all. We can create that same chemotherapy to reverse cancer using our mind, because now even doctors know that cancer is caused by negative energy. Did you know that we don't have cancer in the rainforest? And why? Is it that we are special people? No! Western world people are just like people from the rainforest. They are made of the same ingredients, the same molecules. The problem is the negative energy created here through daily life by people living with stressful schedules, turmoil, jealousy, hate, not enjoying life—all of this. These things create distortions in your positive energy and this can lead you to an illness.

> The mainstream doctors are very powerful, very knowledgeable. But when they don't find a way to heal a person, they just give up. If a person comes to a doctor with a cancer, the first thing they do is say "You have cancer. You have just two months to live." I did some healings on a woman whose doctor told her that she has only two weeks to live. When I saw this woman I knew she was going to live a long time. And she has cancer! She said to me, "Ipu, this cancer will not defeat me. I am going to be the winner." I told her, "The way you are thinking, you are reversing your cancer." Now she is feeling much better. She will probably live twenty or thirty years more, even though the doctor told her blue in the face, that she would not live more than two weeks.[17]

A New Paradigm for Personal Healing

In any discussion of healing it is important to point out that the definition of "health" is dependent upon the particular mythology or belief system of an individual or community. In shamanic philosophy, a healing does not necessarily mean a restoration of physical health. On the contrary, whereas modern medicine tends to see death as a failed healing, in the shamanic worldview, death is often seen as the ultimate healing. Although those of us brought up in the west tend to see death as something fearful to be avoided as long as possible, for the shaman, death is not seen as the end to everything, but rather a necessary and desirable transition that all will make within a lifetime. All shamanic traditions believe in the continuation of the soul after death, which is why, as we have seen, shamans continue to feel connected to those who have lived before, knowing that their essence is still existing in the world. Part of the shaman's role as healer also includes conducting deceased souls to the afterlife after death. As psychopomp, the shaman is uniquely qualified to act as an escort, having made the trip to the realms beyond death each time he or she takes a journey.

Tom Cowan explained to me one day:

> When you ask people who have been working in shamanism a long time how has it changed their lives, one of the things that has come up over and over again is that they feel less fearful of the universe and, therefore, less fearful of death. The "something" that happens after death is a part of the other world that the shaman journeys into and comes back with information and stories about. It's not quite as unknown as it is to people who are not involved in this kind of work.... Shamanism can provide hope for people that death is not as disastrous or as final as it might seem. And if the shaman can cast some new light on the questions life and

death, that might be one of the greatest contributions anyone can make.[18]

Throughout most of this chapter we have looked mainly at healing on an individual, personal level. Although individual healing may certainly be a large part of his or her clientele, the shaman's healing practices involve not just personal healing, but community and planetary healing as well. Besides working with human beings, the shaman may do soul retrievals or extractions for any system that is thrown out of balance. In *Shamanism*, Mircea Eliade noted that, "The same summoning back of the soul is found among the Karen of Burma who, in addition, employ a similar treatment for the 'sickness' of the rice imploring its 'soul' to return to the crop."[19]

Oscar Miro-Quesada believes that planetary healing is even more the task of the shaman than any other kind of healing work. He says:

> More important than being a shamanic healer is to be able to do an offering to the earth. When we repay the earth, we are doing more to restore balance to a neglected part of spirit than we would by being on a path of service to human beings. By doing earth healing rites and ceremonies, you are re-establishing a conscious, awakened, sacred relationship with the earth, allowing all of the unseen world that inhabits it to feel more comfortable to reveal themselves to those who are still asleep. Feed the earth first, and then you will have the strength to go out on the healing path.[20]

Whether the healing is done on a personal, planetary, or community level is, at a point, irrelevant. When viewed from the philosophy of oneness that is the basic tenet of the shamanic path, the healing of one becomes the healing of another, and the healing of the planet is the healing of us all. Recognizing that nothing is separate, that all are interconnected and interdependent, no such action becomes too great or too small. As in Wilhelm's story of the rainmaker, the most profound act of healing we can do for the world around us is to bring our own personal microcosm into a delicate harmonization and resonance with the cosmos.

Exercises

Exercise #14: Daily Energy Inventory

In order to keep track of how they spend their money each week, many people I know keep a finance journal, in which they write down everything they purchase in a day. In this exercise, instead of money you will be inventorying how you disburse your energy on a daily basis. As you go about your day, become conscious of your thought patterns, both negative and positive. How often do you, either intentionally or unintentionally, send negative thoughts such as anger or fear towards another person or yourself? Do you tend to take on another person's problems? Make a note of it in your journal or recorder. Likewise, record positive feelings of love, appreciation, and so on. From what sources do you receive positive energy? What nourishes you, physically, mentally, and spiritually—food, sleep, good conversation with friends, being outdoors? At the end of the week, go back and take inventory of how you spent your energy this week, as well as the ways in which you received (notice that I did not say "took") positive energy from the world around you.

Exercise #15: Turning Shadow to Gold

At the end of Chapter 2, you did free-flow writing exercises aimed at beginning to uncover your shadow. As we have seen in this chapter, once disowned or hidden, these parts become our Achilles' heel, our vulnerable spot that is open for attack. However, if we can embrace these parts of ourselves, and accept them as elements that define who we are, they will not have power over us. Nor can anyone else use these things to deplete our personal power, leaving us vulnerable to energetic attack. The first step to creating personal power is to no longer have anything left for you to defend.

Go back and reread what you wrote while doing the exercise. How deep did you let yourself go in uncovering your shadow? Some things you read may make you feel very uncomfortable. That is good. The shadow is not brought to light willingly. Rather, we are so often filled with the shame of it that we are not willing to look at it for fear of what we will learn about ourselves. Chances are, the harder it is for you to read what you have written, the more it needs to be revealed. Allow yourself to be uncomfortable, but know that this discomfort is unresolved power that can be harnessed for the good. Once you have read through your previous work, begin another journal entry, noting the things that have come up for you, both the themes that are consistent in your free-flow writings, as well as how you felt rereading them. How could someone use these "weaknesses" against you? Find a trusted friend and read them what you have discovered about yourself. Oftentimes when I do this I find that I have built this part of myself up in my mind to be so monstrous that I am sure that my friend will disown me. More often than not, however, I usually find that when I tell the person, as soon as the words are out of my mouth, it no longer seems like such a terrible thing. I am oftentimes met with the response, "So what? I feel like that a lot of the time, too!" Then we can laugh about it. Once the shadow becomes light it does not disappear. Nor should it, for it is part of our Sacred Wound, that which we will work with all of our lives and, believe it or not, that is the basis for our personal power. By acknowledging it, the shadow loses its ability to be used to deplete your personal power. Likewise, recognizing your shadow can help prevent you from sending potentially destructive energy to others.

Exercise #16: A Journey of Healing

The next time you find yourself experiencing pain of any sort, whether it is physical, mental, or emotional, go back to the steps outlined in Chapter 3 and take a journey to the Lower World. Once you are settled in your landscape, ask for help in your healing. A spirit guide may show up with a message for you. Again, do not discount anything that is given to you, as things that happen in these worlds are not bound to the same laws of time, space, or logic as we are used to. Journey to the Lower World and bring back a message about the cause of and/or cure for your particular imbalance. You can even journey on behalf of a friend who is having health concerns. Or use your altar for this purpose by putting a photo or a personal item from the friend and request help from your spirit allies. (Always get permission from that person before you do anything such as this, however). Record your experiences.

Exercise #17: Living in Reverence

Give the gift of service to the earth. This can be as simple as picking up trash along the side of the road, planting a tree, or leaving daily gifts of food out for the spirits of your land. Make a commitment to making a gesture towards the health of the earth each day. No gesture is too small or insignificant.

Carl Hyatt, a very dear friend of mine who has been an invaluable colleague on this spiritual path, had this to say about practicing this kind of reverent gesture towards the earth:

> I have noticed that when I turn my attention in a reverent, honoring way to the natural world—or actually anything—my small, daily, complaining self immediately becomes quiet. I may arrive somewhere to do ceremony preoccupied with things to do, every day worries and pressures. But when I turn to the natural world, or someone I am with in a deeply honoring way, it is as if I call out a part of myself that is always

there but hidden by the "every day mind." I feel it as a visceral shift in my body. It is as if I step through an invisible door that can only be opened with my heart.[21]

How does your own internal state shift after doing this?

Chapter 7

Open Your Ears to the Song of the Universe:[1] Perception and Awareness

Take a moment and look around you. What things—objects, people, beings—do you see around you? Do an inventory and list the things that you see. A tree? A car? A chair? Other people? What smells, sounds, and tastes fill in the spaces of the world around you?

Now ask yourself: How long did it take you to identify each thing, to attach a word or phrase to everything that your senses picked up? For most of the things on your list, recognition was most likely instantaneous. Unless your senses picked up on something that was unfamiliar or out of context, chances are you had a ready-made label to attach to each item. You recognized immediately, for example, that a piece of furniture with four legs, a seat, and a back is called "chair."

Now look once again, this time focusing on just one of the objects or sensations that surround you—for example, the chair. This time, try to look at it beyond an instantaneous labeling of it. Observe the characteristics of this particular chair. Notice the texture of the material from which it is made, the colors and patterns of the fabric, the swirls of wood grain, the shininess or dullness of its plastic or metal parts. Chances are, the longer you made sensory contact with the point of focus, the more that object or sensation revealed itself to you. You may even be surprised at how the most minute detail that you passed over at first glance now seems obvious to you. How has the object or sensation changed for you now that you have connected to it at a deeper level rather than just simply assigning it a perfunctory label such as "chair"?

The world is full of sensory stimuli: objects, people, smells, sounds, tastes, and feelings. They surround us, filling in the spaces of our everyday lives. Although we interact with these facets of reality on a daily basis, we tend to take their existence for granted, entirely unaware of the complex process of awareness and perception that our nervous system goes through in order to make these sensations available to us at all. What many do not realize is that despite the seeming ease with which we incorporate the world around us into our consciousness, the brain is not simply some passive "camera" designed to reflect and record stimuli from the outside world.

On the contrary, as modern physics tells us, we are not discovering a preexisting reality, but rather are participating in its creation in every moment. We know, because science tells us, that the physical world that we obtain sensory data from is very different from the way in which we internalize it. For example, our physical experience of the chair is that it is solid, stable, and completely fixed in space. And yet, as science reveals, matter is really made up of light waves that are translated to the senses as particle. Our perception of sound is based on the frequency of sound vibrations. And so on. Each of us is the co-creator of our reality. Perception must first happen inside of us before it can happen "out there." Though it may seem instantaneous, the act of perception is an elaborate mental process in which the brain and nervous system must engage in processing, decoding, and then translating this data into sensations that help us make practical sense of the world around us. Through this incredible alchemy of the brain, the world goes from a soup of meaningless patterns of energy into a reality full of objects that we then assign labels to such as "chair," "tree," or "car." As Michael Talbot writes in *The Holographic Universe*, "Matter is a kind of habit."[2]

Nor is the process even as clear cut as that. If it were, all the act of perception would result in is a direct translation of outside stimuli. In fact, not all data that is provided to us by the outside world makes it into our conscious awareness. The brain gives us information on a need-to-know basis. As stimuli enter the unconscious, the brain makes instantaneous decisions about what input is necessary to ensure the individual's physical and mental well-being and what can be passed over or ignored. After receiving a stimulus, the brain initially sorts through all the input given in order to find the simplest concept—visual, olfactory, auditory, whatever—to fit the data. Take, for example, the chair (or whatever object or sensation you chose to focus on at the beginning of the chapter). The first time you took note of it, your brain gave you enough conscious information for you to make the perceptual decision that you were, in fact, looking at a chair. Starting at a very young age, we develop mental checklists by which to standardize our world, attach labels to concepts, and quickly and efficiently file them into neat, simple categories and be done with them. The well-meaning parent or teacher will hold a picture of a chair and say, "Look: It has a back, a seat, and four legs. It must be a chair." Trained in this manner, these equations quickly become a part of our unconscious process. Soon enough, every time we become aware of a sensation, our mind does an instantaneous and often unconscious Gestalt: back + seat + legs = chair. Soon we only have to glance at something and we have a ready-made label for it. Only when something is unfamiliar or out of context does our perceptual process slow down enough for us to become aware of it on a conscious level. Then we stop and look at the thing that has caught our attention, mesmerizing us in a moment of focused attention.

Remember the last time a close friend or acquaintance got a new haircut? The first time you saw him or her with it, your initial reaction was probably just to quickly acknowledge that your friend was standing in front of you and move on. But a part of you recognized that something was different about that person, though at first glance you may not have been able to determine exactly what. Thinking back, you can probably remember the process your mind went through trying to sort it all out. Was something *really* different about him or her, or was it just your imagination? Though it probably didn't take too long for you to figure it out, your mind had to sort through various possibilities (a new shirt? a tan?) before it hit on what was different about your friend. Your brain was forced to slow down and experience the process of perception and really "see" your friend in a way you would ordinarily have not.

All this is not to suggest that this process of sorting and filing is somehow wrong. If the brain did not filter out certain information and give us an efficient system of classification, we might be so overloaded with data that we could not put one foot in front of the other. However, although it's both practical and necessary, this kind of perceptual selectivity is limiting and shuts out the greatest portion of magic that is to be found in the world. In *Man and His Symbols*, Carl Jung said, "We have stripped all things of their mystery and numinosity; nothing is holy any longer."[3]

Perceiving Ordinary Reality in a Non-Ordinary Way

In all societies, there are those whose gift is to make us stop and reconnect to the great mystery of the world instead

of passing blindly through it. The truly talented painter of
still lives transforms a bowl of fruit into something beyond a
bowl of fruit. Likewise, the photographer, the actor, and the
poet. One cannot read Pablo Neruda's collection of poems,
Odes to Common Things, without undergoing some kind of
transformation of vision as seemingly unromantic objects such
as soap, socks, or a pair of scissors come to embody a new life
beyond our habitual labeling of them. As is the artist, the
shaman is a master of seeing beyond the "ordinariness" of the
world and into the life that exists within even so-called inanimate objects. The shaman is trained to step back from the
clichés of the consensual world, away from the labels that keep
things frozen and separate, and develop a new relationship
with physical reality as well as his or her interior reality. In
shamanism's animistic view of the world, nothing is ordinary;
everything is sacred and deserving of respect as an integral part
of the greater whole of the cosmos.

At the moment I am sitting in a Turkish café, surrounded
by tapestries. Sitting on the table next to me as I write this is
a paper coffee cup, half full of tea. It is just a paper cup, really
very ordinary; I will throw it away as soon as I have finished
drinking from it. Despite my best attempts, coming from the
cultural upbringing that I do, it is painfully difficult for me to
see it as a conscious entity, something worthy of divine reverence. My conscious experience of it is that it is a dead object
that will soon take up space in some landfill outside of town. I
have a preconceived notion of it, and I struggle to connect to it
on a level that involves slowing down and awakening to the
world with fresh eyes—the eyes of a child and the eyes of the
shaman. Gershon Winkler said to me:

> If I were to be asked to state the fundamental credence
> of Jewish shamanism, I would say that it is about seek-
> ing out the magic of the ordinary. When I ask sha-
> mans from other cultures what it really means to be a

shaman, they say that a shaman is one who trains one-self to step back from the ordinary and to see the magic in it. In fact, the more you step back from trying to figure out the mystery, the more the mystery reveals itself to you.[4]

In the shamanic way of looking at the world, a reality of seemingly "dead" objects becomes reanimated with new life and new significance as intelligences that emanate from the consciousness of the Great Creative Source of the cosmos. As part of his or her training, the shaman, as does the poet, learns to see the universe in a grain of sand. In order to have a conversation with the Creator through the objects and events in his or her world, the shaman learns the language of these intelligences, which, as in a journey or a dream, is made up of metaphor and symbol. The flight of a bird overhead during a pause in a conversation, the chance falling of a leaf, or some synchronicity so strange that it could not have happened by chance—such things act as methods by which spirit and sha-man converse. By learning this language, the shaman becomes fluent in the vocabulary of signs and omens, knowing that all things that exist within the ordinary world are potential mes-sengers of the creative force of the cosmos. Everything is a vehicle for the voice of Spirit, concealed only to those who do not see it as such. Among the Inuit people of Alaska, a person who wants to become a shaman's apprentice might explain to his mentor, "*Takujumaqama*—I come to you because I desire to see."[5,6]

Perceiving Beyond Physical Reality

In addition to filtering out that which is considered "un-necessary" for an organism's immediate survival, the uncon-scious mind also selectively denies access to input or information that does not fit into these standardized categories and there-fore might cause the individual anxiety or emotional unrest.

In other words, that which does not conform to an established and reinforced paradigm of the world is subject to the brain's censorship. Our conscious perception therefore depends if not entirely, then at least to a very significant extent,[7] on what we have been taught to see, hear, smell, taste, or feel. In contemporary culture, children who see spirits or energy fields or anything outside of the "normal" range of perception are often told by well-meaning adults that it is imagination, a dream, not "real." Any information that does not jive with the current model of reality then becomes repressed within them in order to harmonize ourselves with the currently accepted paradigm of the world. Over time, the brain ceases to allow this information into the conscious awareness, passing over any input that is out of the ordinary, out of context. Thus, the world goes from a place of unlimited possibility to one of a carefully modeled construct. The old axiom "seeing is believing" is just as true in the reverse, for believing is also seeing and allows for greater possibilities within the world.

How we perceive reality differs from person to person, culture to culture, and is largely dependent upon our personal or cultural idiosyncrasies, habits, beliefs, and training. Ask two people to describe the same event and you're likely to hear two radically different accounts. On a physical level, perception is just as much a product of training and experience. There are fascinating stories of people blind from birth who have had their sight restored in adulthood. Despite the fact that the individuals were *physically* able to see, their brains had never learned to process the information coming to the eyes. A patient who was shown an orange was unable to tell what it was, or even that it was round, until he was able to touch it. Only after years of training are many of these people able to use their vision in the way that most people do.[8]

Not only is the physical act of perceiving in greater part a learned ability, but how we *apply* the perception that we do have is specialized to suit survival within our environment.

History tells of Magellan's trip around the world in 1519 and how some of the natives that the explorers encountered were physically unable to see the giant ships that sailed into the harbor. As the story goes, it wasn't until the crew got into their longboats that the natives reacted (and with utter terror) to their presence. The explorers later discovered that the size of the ships was so inconceivable to the natives that they could not grasp their existence and therefore did not see them. The explorers had seemingly appeared out of nowhere. In recent years, experiments have validated the idea that the brain's selective processing mechanism "de-selects" input that is outside of one's programming. For example, kittens raised in rooms with only vertical black and white lines on the wall grew up "blind" to horizontal lines and would fall off any small, edge-like step.

It is sobering to think that much of what we "see" (and, likewise, what we don't see) has been interpreted and rearranged by the mind to fit a strict model informed by our upbringing. One might wonder, then, what details of the ordinary world we pass by on a conscious level in order to maintain our firm grasp on reality as we know it. That which does manage to come to conscious awareness is therefore most likely only a fraction of the information about the world that we could potentially access.

Of course, knowing this limitation can be empowering as well. If we accept the idea that reality is, at least to a certain extent, a personal construction, then each of us has the power to change it, to expand the blinders imposed by one's conditioning. For as many doors of perception that can be shut, as many can be opened as well.

For the shaman, learning to open these doors and interact with the ordinary world of existence through non-ordinary means is fundamental to his or her work and, in particular, his or her healing practices. As we have seen, it is through using the ability to perceive psychically that the shaman is able to diagnose illness and "see" the spirits and blockages that are responsible for disrupting the client's physical and/or emotional health. By expanding his or her perceptual state, the shaman can sense things that, in an ordinary state of affairs, remain just below the threshold of awareness filtered out by the logical mind.

Through various means, the shaman learns how to bypass this filtering system and slip into a new state of awareness and perception.

Stopping the Internal Dialogue

Just about all forms and techniques of psychic knowing involved a similar process of quieting the logical mind that keeps one stuck in habitual patterns of thought, thereby opening that part of consciousness that is at all times aware of every and all movements within the cosmos. To achieve this state, all thinking must be dropped, because thinking is antithetical to perceiving. In *Tales of Power* Carlos Castaneda called this process "stopping the internal dialogue."[9]

Brooke Medicine Eagle, Native American teacher and author of *Buffalo Woman Comes Singing*, agrees:

> It is really important for people to find a way of silencing the mind, of stilling the inner voices that are constantly jabbering and calling for attention. That chatter keeps us hooked into old ways of thinking. The idea is to get you to stop talking to yourself; to stop paying attention to the voices that say "Sit-down-shut-up-you-don't-know-anything-you-shouldn't-do-that-this-is-too-hot-this-is-too-cold-no-there-aren't-faeries-there-aren't-elves-there-aren't-devas."[10]

When this internal silence is achieved, one finds a Zen-like still point from which to access the world beyond the world, a place in which one's consciousness resonates to a vibrational state in which one can access that which resides just outside the grasp of normal consciousness. By quieting the internal chatter and holding this space of silence, one becomes a receiver of stimuli—not an interpreter or manipulator of it—and a mirror of existence in its purest form. I discussed this concept with Ken Eagle Feather of the Toltec tradition.

> It is the inherent nature of humans to have this thing called "self-reflection." Reality itself is just a mass amount of self-reflection. When we define our world, we are really just reflecting, and then producing from that reflection. You have to be connected with the world, otherwise the feelings that you have are going to be reflective. They are going to occur as a state of projection, of what your internal state is. So you are not connected to the world, you're just connected to yourself. When you stop the internal dialogue and connect with the world through feeling, you become inundated, saturated, with a whole new set of data.... The world is connected to the universe, and because you are now connected with the world you become part of the universe. And that process, the journey of achieving that connection is the work of the [shaman].[11]

To become one with the world, to achieve a state of mergence, remains an important aspect of the shaman's shift of consciousness into a state of expanded awareness. By stepping outside of the belief systems and habitual thinking that dictate ordinary—and often limited—modes of perception, the shaman becomes a mirror of the world in its most uncorrupted form. When this is achieved, the perceiver and the perceived become as one, establishing what D.H. Lawrence called a "pure relationship between ourselves and the living universe about us." He wrote, "This is how I 'saved my soul' by accomplishing a pure relationship between me and another person, me and other people, me and a nation, me and a race of men, me and the animals, me and the trees or flowers, me and the earth, me and the skies and sun and stars, me and the moon: an infinity of pure relations, big and little."[12] In this state, a relationship between subject and object is created where the boundaries between inner and outer no longer exist. Psychologists call this "identification participation."

Mike and Nancy Samuels wrote in *Seeing with the Mind's Eye*:

> The feeling of identification-participation causes a person to be less involved with himself as an entity separate from the world around him. He goes beyond the boundaries, the limitations of his physical body, beyond the awareness of his personality.... He no longer sees the image in terms of categories or labels, functions or expectations. Desire and attachment disappear, and, in that sense, he sees the image for itself, not as it relates to him. Perhaps for the first time since childhood he sees the image free of learned habits, cultural biases, secondary gain. He is aware of the whole and all its parts, the inside and the outside, the generality and the particulars. Time and space disappear. At that point there is no separation between him and the image; there's just your experience of his psychic awareness.
>
> As a person approaches this experience, certain unusual things happen to him. He receives new information in the form of images, ideas, feelings and sensations. This information is different from the information of learned habits and biases. This new knowledge and understanding may appear to come from outside of him, in much the same way that dreams and visions seemed to come from outside. A person does not so much summon the information as it comes to him and he receives it. A person who has this experience feels it unites him with the universe. He feels he is a part of creation, rather than an observer of it. And the information he receives is pure, tied to the most universal of rhythms.

This purity of vision, this one-pointedness of mind, is associated with tremendous energy surrounding both the visualizer and the image, and the unity of the two.[13]

Adjusting One's Perceptual Apparatus

Besides stopping the internal dialogue and silencing in the mind to become a pure receiver, the neophyte shaman may be trained with exercises aimed at relearning how to see, both physiologically and psychically. In the book *Shamanic Wisdom Keepers*, Native American shaman Jamie Sams tells the story of her training, in which her teachers helped her develop her perceptual awareness by sitting and observing the world without blinking for up to eight hours:

> My teachers, when they started me, would sit me on one of the busiest intersections in a big city in Mexico. And they would make me sit without blinking for about five minutes. And maybe in five minutes 150 people would walk by and they'd say: "How many people walked by that were wearing pink?" And that was the first lesson. And so you extend your perception peripherally with your eyes. You have to also perceive every single thing around you in a different way. They worked me up to sitting eight hours without moving, blinking, twitching. And then they upped the gradient. Like asking: "How many people walked by who had a disability?" And of course they knew the answers! "How many people walked by who had a life-threatening disease and a hole in their dreaming body?" "How many people walked by who were holding a death wish?" "How many people walked by who were fulfilled and happy?" And on and on until I could take it all in. It was observing the obvious and then observing energy—the intangible and the physical together.[14]

Other similar sorts of physical adjustments may help the shaman-in-training learn to perceive the world in an altered state of awareness. I had a teacher who would bemoan the fact that his students could be staring straight into the woods and not see the herd of deer that stood just beyond the tree line in plain sight. In order to survive, hunter-gatherers maintained an expanded state of awareness that could perceive the smallest motion on the landscape around them, could tell the direction of game by the smell of the wind, and could hear the rustling of the stalking carnivore behind them. In contrast, modern people do not have a need for such expansive perceptual acuity. As comedian George Carlin said, "All that is left of the hunt is the supermarket." Modern culture is experiencing a kind of perceptual atrophy. Instead of this wide range of awareness, modern man plows through the world, looking straight ahead at some fixed point on the horizon. With this laserlike focus, we have accomplished many things. We can set and achieve goals that allow us to build ships to fly to the moon, drive to the store, and balance our checkbooks. But with this tunnel vision, modern people have also strapped on a very narrow set of blinders that cuts out the greater portion of the world around us.

In order to counteract this limitation, this same teacher teaches his students a technique called "Wide Angle Vision." This exercise is much like looking at one of those Magic Eye pictures, in which, in order to see the 3-D image hidden under the computer-generated patterns, one must soften the focus and allow the eyes to take in the entire picture at once instead of isolating specific parts. By adjusting one's focus in this way, one's perception is given a wider range of awareness. By doing this exercise, not only can one physically see more of the world, which is important in itself, but I've heard it said that going into wide-angle vision causes the brain to jump instantly into an alpha brainwave state. In this state of expanded awareness and meditation, one can bring the dream mind to everyday, waking consciousness.

Through repeated practice of seeing the world in an altered way, the shaman blazes new trails in his or her perceptual apparatus, which, as new data is incorporated, remodels his or her worldview as well. The mind is thus stretched to incorporate new data about the world rather than sticking to old inventories and checklists. Over time, the shaman's awareness of the world becomes continually expanded as he or she integrates this information as part of a new reality.

As part of his training, Ken Eagle Feather's teacher don Juan (of Carlos Castaneda fame) would constantly and purposefully throw his student's perceived perceptions of the world out of balance in order to expand his visual paradigms. He told me:

> What he would do is throw me out of whack to the point where I would emotionally and physically lose my orientation to the world. I would have a loss of meaning. I'd be out for a walk and, in my typical days of connecting to the world, I'd be not paying attention to anything. Don Juan would appear in front of me, clear out of the blue. The first several times I saw him materialize, I could not perceive of him just stepping out of thin air. That was way beyond my scope, so at first I would just see him walking toward me like you'd see anybody walking toward you. Once my body was able to process that kind of data, I would literally see him step out of thin air.[15]

I stumbled upon the possibilities of this space of silence and altered awareness one day entirely by accident. Several seasons ago, I worked as one of three caretakers of a large piece of property in northern Massachusetts. It was November, one of those perfect New England fall days when one's senses are overloaded with an explosion of colors, sounds, and smells. I was working alone near a recently drained pond, lost in the rhythm of raking leaves and the deep stillness of the crisp morning. Out of the corner of my eye, I saw movement from the direction of the pond. I turned my head to look and saw a medium-sized wild cat—what looked like a lynx—walking across the empty pond. This in itself would be strange, as wild cats of any kind are not common in that area. Even stranger, however, was that the cat did not seem to be made of solid matter. The best way I can explain it is that it was as if it was made out of a very liquid, clear gelatin—nearly solid matter, but rippling like water that has assumed a form. The Jell-O Cat paid no attention to me; it just walked across the mud. A moment later, it disappeared from sight, vanishing back into nothingness.

The entire sighting lasted probably no more than a few seconds, but in that time I could literally feel the information being sent around my brain, looking for a place in which to settle. It first went to my logical mind, but my logical mind wanted nothing to do with it. The image had no place in its reality, and so it rejected it. Fortunately, through my spiritual practice, my belief system had been widened enough that my spirit mind had enough say in the matter to be able to accept and integrate this information into my consciousness. Had I not been doing this work, the image most likely would have been censored completely by my logical mind and not been registered consciously at all. Even so, the first moments after the cat disappeared, I had to remind myself over and over not to doubt what I'd seen.

What the Jell-O Cat was or where it came from, I do not know. I won't even try to guess. As of yet, I have not had an experience like that again, though I would like to. As so often is the case, the harder I try to re-create that elusive space—the combination of inner silence and heightened awareness—the harder it has been to do so. But as with finding the shell in the woods, the experiences opened up, even for the briefest moment, a whole new world of possibility and magic with which to relate to the world around me.

Exercises

Exercise #18: Stopping the Internal Dialogue

This may be the most important exercise in the book, for virtually all spiritual practice is about silencing the mind so that one's consciousness, one's awareness, can be a pure channel with which to engage with both this and the unseen world. To a certain extent, "Stopping the Internal Dialogue" is what you have been working towards all along as you prepare yourself and your space before each exercise.

There are numerous exercises for creating this space, and almost all of them involve some kind of technique to reconnect one to one's breath. Breath is not just essential for physical survival, but the vehicle for transforming consciousness, for the breath and the mind are intimately connected. Singing and chanting are common practices among many, if not most, religious and spiritual traditions, used as ways of sending prayers to the sacred through the vehicle of breath. The word *inspiration*, in fact, means both "inhalation" and "stimulation of the mind or emotions to a high level of feeling or activity."[16] When focused in an intentional way, breath becomes the means by which anyone can begin to establish resonance and mergence with the world.

This exercise will help connect you to your breath. First, completely empty your lungs of air. Now, inhale slowly to the count of 12. Hold the breath for a count of 12. Exhale for a count of 12. Do not hold the breath after the exhale, but go immediately into the next inhale, again for the count of 12. As you get more comfortable with the exercise, increase the count from 12 to 15, then to 18, and then 20. At 20 you are breathing at a rate of one breath per minute.

Once you have gotten used to this rhythm and can do it easily and without thought, try this: As you breathe, imagine yourself inhaling light. As you hold the breath, visualize the body separating the energy of the air and releasing it into your body, seeping into you the way a sponge soaks up water into each of its pores. As you exhale out, release negativity and heaviness that you carry with you.

Exercise #19: Life Is but a Dream

This is one of my favorite exercises. It is incredibly simple to do, and I find that it almost instantaneously propels me out of habitual consciousness and into an altered state that I can use to explore the world around me.

When we wake up from a dream and think back on it, most of us try to determine what the dream means. When we dream of a black cat sitting next to a pot of geraniums, we think, "What does that cat mean?" "Is there significance to the fact that it is black, rather than white or calico?" Immediately we know if there is or isn't. Carl Jung once said, as Bettina Knapp wrote in *Anais Nin*, "Proceed from the dream outward."[17] In this exercise we will do just that by bringing the dream mind to everyday consciousness.

Prepare yourself and your space. Allow your eyes not to focus on anything; just have extended vision. Imagine that the world around you is really a dream. Slowly walk around, touch and smell things, use all your senses; approach the world as if in a lucid waking state. You will be amazed how colors seem brighter, objects and sensations more vivid and more radiant. Listen to the world around you. What is the furthest sound that you can hear? Extend your consciousness as far as possible, then slowly move it in towards you, bringing it all in towards you as if gathering all the sounds and sensations in your arms. Bring it all inside you until it fills you.

When I do this it always amazes me how new the world seems to me. Suddenly, as in a dream, nothing can be taken for granted, for just by its existence it becomes imbued with significance. By going into this exercise deeply, one can establish a perceptual state similar to what one experiences after ingesting a hallucinogenic drug or plant spirit. The beauty of this is that it is safer, cheaper, and, of course, legal. Most importantly, one can move in and out of this state at will. Try creating a piece of art in this state—for example, a poem, or a painting. You may be amazed at what details of the world reveal themselves to you that you might have ordinarily passed over.

Exercise #20: Opening Your Ears to the Song of the Universe

The following is another exercise given to me by Cheryl Krisko. It is absolutely beautiful and appropriate considering what we have discussed in this chapter about "hearing" the song of the universe. This is an exercise in which you will "receive" a medicine song. The "song" may be used to call upon the energies of the place when needed and can help you embody a variety of frequencies at once. It also seriously opens and alters one's perception.

Give yourself a time allotment, anywhere from 45 minutes to four hours. Bring a blanket, a pen or pencil, a notebook, and anything else that you may need for comfort or safety, such as a jacket or pillow. Open yourself to the sounds around you and for the duration of your time *write down every sound that you hear*. Be descriptive of the sound itself. In other words, rather than writing "two crows, a lawnmower, chickadee, winds in the grasses," write *exactly* the sounds you hear, as in: "caw caw caw caw crk crk br br brm dee dee chick dee dee dee fwee hah fweehah shsh shhhh wishshsh wishshsh." At the end of your allotted time, close your notebook, thank your spot, and leave. Notice any changes in your hearing abilities and your sensitivity to sounds. At another time, on another day, revisit your notebook and see what you notice. Do you remember your experience—what it looked like, smelled like, felt like? Now look at the words you wrote and notice rhythms and patterns, especially those that express your experience. When you are ready, construct a short poem or medicine song using some of those sounds and patterns. Learn your song by heart and use it in the future to summon the voluptuous vibrations of your experience of your spot.

Afterword

Shamanism:
The Path of the Heart

Not long ago, I attended an art exhibit with a friend of mine. Amidst the various pieces on display was a huge, life-sized, incredibly realistic model of a tribal man draped in animal skins, staring out at the world from behind an ornate mask. The figure was so penetrating that I could almost hear the beating of drums in the distance. Aptly, the work was entitled *Shaman*.

My friend pointed to the sculpture. "There," he said, almost in triumph. "That is what a *real* shaman looks like. Not those white people you study with!"

Leaving me with that comment, he moved on to the next piece. At first I was annoyed. Then I found myself getting angry enough to entertain an impulse to throw my martini glass at the back of his head. It stuck with me, and I spent the rest of the evening and a part of the next day stewing about it. And then I realized *why* I was so angry. His comment had touched a raw nerve in me, something I had been struggling with for quite some time. A part of me had always wondered if he was right. As relative newcomers to this work, we in the west may find ourselves fumbling our way through this exploration of shamanism as a spiritual path. We try a little of this and a little of that, learning the techniques and traditions of certain cultures, creating others from our own authentic interactions with spirit, doing what we can to learn to bypass the cultural conditioning that limits our experience of the world.

With each workshop, book, or mystical experience, we take on the challenge of retraining ourselves to expand the limitations of our belief systems and consciousness in order to see the world through indigenous eyes. And this is not easy in a culture that very much denies our ability to do this. As a result, we may feel unequal to the task. And so we are left wondering: How can a spiritual tradition born out of people living close to the earth become a viable spiritual practice for those living in an environment so physically and ideologically different from the one in which shamanism emerged? It had always concerned me that as a westerner I might never truly be able to understand the vision of the shaman. So, then, what right did I have to take these ancient traditions and attempt to incorporate them into my own spiritual practice?

I have heard this same doubt expressed by many westerners on this path. My friend's comment reflects a collective prejudice that exists within our culture about our own abilities to do this work. It has been my experience that, with a few exceptions, the indigenous teachers of shamanic cultures do not carry this same bias that coming from a 21st-century technical culture disqualifies one from following these traditions. Put more bluntly, there is nothing about being white and/or "modern" that excludes one from contacting God. As my own teachers have reminded me, no matter what part of the world each of us originates from, no matter who our most recent ancestors were or how or where we live today, each one of us descends from shamanic ancestry. No matter how far we feel we have moved away from that legacy, each one of us has the ability to reconnect to that part of ourselves that extends beyond our physical selves—the part that is free to explore the cosmos and gain knowledge and insight from our allies in the spirit world. That knowledge is within us, however hidden under layers of cultural conditioning it may be. Each one of us can step outside of the Newtonian vision of the world that we have adopted and access the infinite.

During one of our talks, Ipupiara Makunaiman reminded me:

> When the Creator created us, he put in our DNA, in our cellular makeup, all the information that we need. We are like a hard drive in a computer. I remember the first time I had a computer in front of me. I knew that the computer had some programs in there, but where were they? I had no idea how to access those files until someone showed me. When we are born, we are born with all that data stored inside of us. When we wake up, when we have that awakening to work with the spirits and to work with these teachings, the first thing we have to learn is how to retrieve that data.[1]

Learning to retrieve that data then becomes the task of anyone coming to this path. That is especially true for those of us in non-indigenous cultures, faced with the added challenge of changing a belief system that is based on a significantly different world view than the one that shamanism offers us. When asked how far someone coming from a non-indigenous setting could go with this work, Oscar Miro-Quesada said, "The furthest we'll ever have to travel is from our heads to our hearts."[2]

Shamanism as a spiritual practice has been called many times the "Path of the Heart." The heart as an organ has been regarded by various spiritual and religious traditions over time as being the part of the body that contains the soul. Whether or not the physical heart is literally the seat of consciousness, I haven't a clue. But whether actual or symbolic, calling shamanism the "Path of the Heart" refers to a practice dedicated to reconnecting us to the part of the self that is at all times connected to the innate wisdom of the cosmos within and around us and that allows for unlimited possibilities within the world. We can look at the heart as our axis mundi, the center of our own personal world, our inner accessing point to the rest of creation. By opening up and allowing the heart to speak and see and hear clearly, we can gain access to all worlds, to all times, and to all states of consciousness. It is from this point that the shaman establishes his or her unique vision and, paradoxically, finds his or her oneness with the rest of creation at the same time. For the purpose of this book I have been calling that accessing point one's "spirit mind," but an even more appropriate term for it might be "love." In fact, the moment of this connection is sometimes described as coming to the shaman as a surge of energy through the body very similar to the feeling of being in love. The writings of mystics and shamans from many traditions are scattered with the transcendent experience being likened very literally to being taken by a lover.

It is hard to make such a statement without sounding cliché or overly sentimental, but that love energy is the cornerstone of all shamanic work. Love is the root of the "pure relationship" with the world that D.H. Lawrence spoke of. Without that energy flowing unimpeded, reality becomes a frozen, immovable place, and we engage with the world only on the most superficial level. And by love I do not *necessarily* mean love as the emotional connection between two people, although that is one manifestation of it. Certainly, I have found that in moments of deep love for another person I have experienced great intuitive knowing. That same feeling may arise when one is faced with a beauty and awe that reaches into the core of oneself and opens one up to a sense of mystery and connection with all things. We've all experienced it at one time or another when watching a sunset, seeing a painting, or hearing a piece of music or poem that touches and moves us to the point of opening us up to some deeply hidden truth within. We feel this as an "awakening." In that moment, no matter how brief, one has been touched by the numinous, the source of all intuition, wisdom, and power. This is the place that all healing comes from and is the greatest link to our allies in the spirit world. The shaman makes his or her way there in the initiation and must source from it thereafter. It is the entranceway to the center pillar from which all worlds emanate and merge into one, a place beyond time and space that the shaman accesses through ecstasy and ritual. By establishing a resonance with the energy of the heart—love—one becomes a pure channel for interacting with and perceiving the world around you.

Even more than training the student in various rituals and techniques, the greatest role of the teacher in this, and perhaps any spiritual path, becomes helping the student connect more fully to the wisdom of his or her own heart. Indeed, as I have heard many teachers say in one way or another, "I am not here to teach you anything. I am here to help you remember." Every diagram of the cosmos, every spiritual system, becomes a map to lead the seeker back to this dynamic source of knowledge. These models are essential to the practice and act as signposts along the journey from which one may receive guidance. These systems are irreplaceable in their ability to act as a bridge between the logical and the intuitive. The danger in adopting any system, however, is in mistaking the model for the real thing. Just as the science student in a freshman chemistry class realizes that, although for teaching purposes the electron pairs are often represented as discrete points or dots, this is not actually the way it looks in its physical form. In this same way, the student of any spiritual system should aim to transcend all metaphor, all logical reference, in order to experience the pure relationship between the heart and the cosmos.

Because this connection transcends all powers of human expression, any belief system is but an approximation used to convey an idea or experience. The ideas presented in this book are in no way absolutes. Shamanism exists in a place beyond language or explanation and is impossible to define in any way that is more than a clever metaphor. Although a good tool in the beginning stages, explanations have a tendency to pin ideas down like bugs under glass, rendering them immobilized, frozen, unchanging—essentially "dead." By doing this, one once again goes from pure experience to habitual labeling. Instead, these metaphors should act as training wheels, ideas for the logical mind to chew on while the heart, that primordial center of intuition and knowledge, remembers and understands.

A true teacher seeks to help the student empower him or herself through connecting to this heart space, not to rely on them or any "guru" as a substitute for one's personal experience. Unfortunately, students and teachers of all spiritual paths, including shamanism, often forget this. Abuses of power happen all too frequently in this work. Perhaps it is because of our prejudice against ourselves that we sometimes have the tendency to give our personal power away to someone who we feel is more "holy" than we are. Throughout this book, I have somewhat glorified the shaman as being almost semi-divine in his or her abilities and wisdom. In practice, of course, this must be taken with a grain of salt and a good dose of reality thrown in. As the rest of us, they are human—no more, no less. If they are at all like gods, then, like all of us, they are more analogous to the gods and goddesses of ancient mythology, divine personalities who, in spite of exceptional abilities in the spiritual realm, are just as prone to acts of stupidity and vanity as they are wisdom and benevolence. As a friend of mine says, "I've met a lot of shamans, but I haven't met any saints yet." Or, as Mayan teacher and author Martin Prechtel points out, "[Shamans] are not holy people. They are people in love with the sacred."[3]

The most important aspect of this work is to regain a belief in ourselves and, more specifically, in our abilities to connect to the unseen, to the numinous that exists within and without. The teachings of any one person or system should therefore not be relied upon as strict dogma, but rather as a jumping-off place from which to dive into a deeper, more personal experience of Spirit. We have all seen the icons of power in our society from various walks of life—spiritual, political, athletic—brought low by personal scandal when they have used the power entrusted to them indulgently or inappropriately. There is a delicate balance between trusting your teacher to act as a guide through these realms and abdicating one's own sensibilities and responsibility. In the end, it is our own inner sense that we must follow as guide, and a true teacher leads us to drink from the source of our own innate wisdom.

This, of course, is easier said than done. To reclaim this power and make the transition from logic to intuitive knowing involves a dramatic leap in consciousness. Sometimes this transformation comes gently and in small steps over the course of a lifetime. At other times, the individual may be dramatically (and traumatically) propelled into a radically altered state. Because of this, the path of the shaman is not one to be undertaken lightly.

However, although this work is challenging, I have come to believe that the ultimate goal of anyone following the path of the shaman, or any spiritual practice for that matter, is to continue whittling away at that part of the self that keeps us locked into limiting belief systems. To free ourselves from these constraints is the greatest gift we can give ourselves, both as individuals and as a culture as a whole. Having dropped the boundaries created by that part of the self that keeps us bound to our clichés and separates us from each other and the world around us, we can reconnect to the infinite. Once freed from the "impossible," that which is possible—both for the world and ourselves—becomes endless. From there we are able to roam the worlds of spirit unimpeded, engaging with the world in its totality and discovering for ourselves the unlimited healing powers of cosmos and consciousness.

Chapter Notes

Introduction

1. Some researchers believe shamanism may even date back as far as 100,000 years or more.

2. Tom Cowan, *Fire in the Head: Shamanism and the Celtic Spirit* (Harper San Francisco, 1993) p. 30.

3. Today in the west, words such as *neo-shaman* and *shamanic practitioner* have emerged as a way of describing an individual who is not a native of any one tradition, but uses the philosophy and practices of shamanism in his or her daily life and/or work. While the importance of this division depends on the individual, these semantic distinctions can serve to show respect for a title of honor that implies a lifetime of dedication and training.

Chapter 1

1. Don Campbell (Editor), *Music and Miracles: A Companion to Music: Physician for Time to Come* (Wheaton, Ill.: Quest Books, 1992), p. 58.

2. Robert Gass, *Chanting: Discovering the Spirit in Sound* (New York: Bantam Doubleday, 2000), pp. 35–36.

3. Refers to the phenomenon that occurs when one tuning fork begins to tone, and another that is near it will begin to vibrate at the same frequency and with the same sound.

4. Although this concept may be hard to grasp by western minds used to thinking in Newtonian terms, over the last 50 years, along with the discovery of the new physics, the question of the existence of parallel universes—worlds that exist side by side along with our own—has taken on renewed interest well beyond speculation.

5. Mircea Eliade, *Shamanism: Archaic Techniques of Ecstasy*, trans. Willard R. Trask, Bollingen series, vol. 76 (Princeton, N.J.: Princeton Univ. Press, 1972), p. 205.

6. Sarangerel, *Riding Windhorses: A Journey into the Heart of Mongolian Shamanism* (Rochester, Vt.: Destiny Books, 2000), p. 12.

7. Michael Harner, *The Way of the Shaman* (New York: Bantam Books, 1982), p. 34. Originally published 1980 by Harper & Row.

8. A form of matter in which a particle has the opposite properties of its counterpart. Scientists are discovering that there are antimatter counterparts for every particle known today.

9. Gary F. Morning, *The Complete Idiot's Guide to Understanding Einstein* (Indianapolis: Alpha Books, 1999), p. 10.

10. Tom Cowan, oral interview, June 30, 2000.

11. Sarangerel, *Riding Windhorses*, p. 13.

12. John G. Neihardt, *Black Elk Speaks* (New York: Simon and Schuster, 1975), pp. 22–47.

13. Eliade, *Shamanism*, p. 191.

14. Machaelle Small Wright, *Behaving as if the God in All Things Mattered: A New Age Ecology* (Jeffersonton, Va.: Perelandra, 1987), p. 101.

15. A phrase coined by Carlos Castaneda to refer to the physical-material realm; things that exist in time and space as they are perceived and understood in normal waking state of consciousness.

16. Mary Pope Osborne, *Favorite Norse Myths* (New York: Scholastic, Inc., 1996), p. 4.

17. David Adams Leeming, *A Dictionary of Creation Myths* (Oxford University Press, 1996), p. 46.

18. Although not commonly recognized as a "shamanic" tradition, ancient Jewish spiritual wisdom is full of teachings regarding the four directions, animal allies, and working with the spirit-in-all-things in order to heal and gain knowledge. For further information about this tradition, I highly recommend the book *Magic of the Ordinary: Recovering the Shamanic in Judaism* by Gershon Winkler.

19. According to Winkler, the word for North is *t'safon*, which means "hidden," indicating it as the place of mystery. West is *ma'arav*, the "place of blending," as in the place where day blends into night. South is *neggev*, which means "cleansing" or *da'rom*, the "place of rising." East is both *kedem*, "beginning," and *meez'rach*, "from the place of shining."

20. Because of these discrepancies between traditions, I believe it is important at a certain point along the path for the individual to find one specific tradition and stick to it. Without roots in a specific tradition helping one to define, as in this case, each of the four directions, the individual can become spiritually "lost in space."

21. Puma Quispe, oral interview, April 12, 2002.

22. Ibid.

23. Alex Stark, oral interview, February 6, 2000.

24. Ibid.

25. Brant Secunda, oral interview, May 3, 2000.

26. Jean Chevalier and Alain Gheerbrant, *The Penguin Dictionary*

of Symbols, trans. John Buchanan-Brown (London: Penguin Books, 1996), p. 1022.

Chapter 2

1. This outline of the five stages of initiation is loosely based on Evelyn Underhill's description of the development of mystical consciousness, which is detailed in her book, *Mysticism*.

2. Piers Vitebsky, *The Shaman: Voyages of the Soul, Trance, Ecstasy, and Healing from Siberia to the Amazon* (Living Wisdom series; Little, Brown and Company, 1995), p. 57.

3. Oscar Miro-Quesada, oral interview, July 25, 2000.

4. A psychoactive cactus species containing mescaline, usually found in the Andes.

5. Eliade, *Shamanism*, p. 140.

6. Tom Cowan, *Fire in the Head*, pp. 14–16.

7. Larry G. Peters, Ph.D., "The 'Calling,' the Yeti, and the Ban Jhankri ('Forest Shaman') in Nepalese Shamanism," *The Journal of Transpersonal Psychology* 29, no. 1 (1997): 10.

8. Bob Curran, *An Encyclopedia of Celtic Mythology* (New York: McGraw-Hill/Contemporary Books, 2000), p. 47.

9. Joseph Campbell, *The Hero with a Thousand Faces* (New Jersey: Princeton University Press, reprint edition, 1972), p. 78.

10. Miro-Quesada, July 25, 2000.

11. Medicine Grizzlybear Lake, *Native Healer: Initiation into an Ancient Art* (Wheaton, Ill., Theological Publishing House, 1991), p. 10.

12. Secunda, May 3, 2000.

13. Peters, "The 'Calling'..." p. 55.

14. Miro-Quesada, May 3, 2000.

15. Larry G. Peters, Ph.D., "Mystical Experience in Tamang

Shamanism," *ReVision: The Journal of Consciousness and Transformation* 13, no. 2 (Fall 1990): 78.

16. For the purpose of this book, shamans acting with the intent to harm or take advantage of others are called "sorcerers."

17. Joseph Campbell, *The Power of Myth* (New York: Anchor Books, 1988) p.151.

Chapter 3

1. *The New Encyclopedia Britannica*, Volume 4, 2002. Encyclopedia Britannica, Inc. p. 359.

2. In some cultures, such as those of Tibetan Bon shamanism and some forms of shamanic technique originating in parts of Africa, the ecstatic state is commonly caused by spirit possession without soul flight, an "indwelling" rather than an "outgoing" in which the shaman travels outward to the spiritual realms. Although possession often implies that the individual is under the control of the spirits, in these practices, the shaman is still able to remain in control of his or her ecstatic state.

3. Evelyn Underhill, *Mysticism: A Study in the Nature and Development of Spiritual Consciousness* (Mineola, N.Y.: Dover Publications, 2002; originally published in 1911): p. 71.

4. A phrase coined by Michael Harner in his book *The Way of the Shaman* to refer to the altered states of consciousness experienced by the shaman during his or her journeys into the spirit world. I use the term as a means of differentiating the shaman's ecstatic flight from those of other ecstatics, such as mystics and spiritualists.

5. Ralph Metzner, Ph.D., "Ayahuasca and the Greening of Human Consciousness," *Shaman's Drum* (Fall 1999): p. 17.

6. Ibid.

7. Ibid.

8. Ibid, p. 18.

9. Harner, *The Way of the Shaman*, p. 56.

10. Michael Talbot, *The Holographic Universe* (New York: HarperCollins, 1991), p. 67.

11. Talbot, *The Holographic Universe*, p. 69.

12. Eliade, *Shamanism*, p. 417.

13. Ibid.

14. According to Michael Harner, a "nagual" refers alternately to both a guardian animal spirit and the shaman who transforms into that animal. In the Mexican shamanic tradition, another word for "shaman."

15. In this same interview, Castaneda defined "glosses" as "a system of perception and language."

16. Sam Keen, "Sorcerer's Apprentice," *Psychology Today*, December 1972, p. 98.

17. Holger Kalweit, *Dreamtime & Inner Space: The World of the Shaman* (Boston: Shambala, 1988), pp. 112, 117, 118.

18. Jim Robbins, *A Symphony in the Brain: The Evolution of the New Brain Wave Biofeedback* (New York: Grove Press, 2000), p. 19.

19. Andrew Neher, "Auditory Driving Observed with Scalp Electrodes in Normal Subjects." *Electroencephalography and Clinical Neurophysiology* 13 (1961): 449–451.

20. Robbins, *A Symphony in the Brain*, p. 161.

21. A still-controversial science in which electronically produced signals are used to quantify the electrical information from a person's brain, often as a way of helping the individual control otherwise unconscious physiological processes.

22. Robbins, *A Symphony in the Brain*, p. 7.

23. Ibid, p. 68.

24. Rabbi Gershon Winkler, oral interview, April 4, 2000.

25. Although through the course of the book I will refer to the perceptions that come to the shaman during the duration of the journey as "images," it is important to note that not all journeyers gather information in the form of mental pictures. For some people the symbolic language of spirit will come through the body in the form of, for example, a kinesthetic response. The manner in which the information comes through depends entirely on the individual's particular receptivity and inherent strengths. Although there is no hierarchy in the sensory experience, the more well-rounded the journey, the better. Highly skilled shamans are said to not only have a single response system, but are able to use all five senses during their journeys.

26. Malidoma Somé, oral interview, September 19, 2000.

27. Ivan Lissner, *Man, God, and Magic*, (New York: Putnam's Sons, 1958), p. 15.

28. Brant Secunda, oral interview, May 3, 2000.

29. Oscar Miro-Quesada, oral interview, November 1, 2000.

30. Tapes and CDs specifically created for Shamanic Journeying are available and include a "call-back" signal recorded into them in order to alert you to when you should come back from the journey.

Chapter 4

1. Eliade, *Shamanism*, p. 108.

2. *Encyclopedia Brittanica*, p. 541.

3. Eliade, *Shamanism*, p. 6.

4. Malidoma Somé, *The Healing Wisdom of Africa: Finding Life Purpose through Nature, Ritual, and Community* (New York: Tarcher/Putnam, 1998), p. 81.

5. Rabbi Gershon Winkler, oral interview, April 14, 2000.

6. Sandra Ingerman, oral interview, June 14, 2000.

7. Although I have made a distinction between the spirit allies of each of the three realms, it is important to remember that these are not fixed designations. Spirit allies can inhabit any one or more of the three realms as well as travel back and forth freely between them.

8. Secunda, oral interview, May 3, 2000.

9. Tom Cowan, oral interview, July 18, 2000.

10. A term taken from Robert Heinlein's classic, *Stranger in a Strange Land*, in which the hero has the ability to merge with the pattern of something, know it from the inside, and change it from the inside by directed intent.

11. Serge Kahili King, oral interview, November 15, 2000.

12. Erik Gonzalez, oral interview, September 7, 2000.

13. Also called *totems* by many Native American traditions, *familiars* in the European tradition, and *nagual* by Central American shamans.

14. Eliade, *Shamanism*, p. 94.

15. Lissner, *Man God and Magic*, p. 279.

16. This respect for animals as a means of accessing the divine is found in other sources as well. Chapter Twelve in the Book of Job says, "Ask now the beasts and they shall tell you. Ask the birds in the sky and they shall guide you. The earth, she shall teach you. The fishes in the sea, they shall direct you."

17. Stephen Larsen, *The Mythic Imagination: The Quest for Meaning through Personal Mythology* (Rochester, Vt.: Inner Traditions, 1996), p. 159.

18. Sarangerel, *Riding Windhorses*, p. 52.

19. Kalweit, *Dreamtime & Inner Space*, p. 127.

20. Winkler, April 14, 2000.

21. *www.alexstark.com/articles.html*. "The Spirit World."

Chapter 5

1. This is not to imply that the rituals of other religious traditions do not have a profound and lasting effect on the consciousness of the individual. Here, however, I am making a distinction between what could be called a "ritual participant" and a "ritual observer."

2. Somé, *The Healing Wisdom of Africa*, p. 165.

3. Margot Adler, *Drawing Down the Moon: Witches, Druids, Goddess-Worshippers, and Other Pagans in America Today* (Boston: Beacon Press, 1979, 1986), p. 161.

4. Larry G. Peters, Ph.D., "The Day the Deities Return: The Janai Purnima Pilgrimage of Tamang Shamans," *Shaman's Drum*, no. 52, 1999, p. 42.

5. Such as in the case of the Achilpa, a nomadic tribe from Australia who would always carry a sacred pole with them to reflect the axis mundi so that they would never be far from the center and therefore can remain in communication with the spirit world. (From Eliade's *The Sacred and the Profane*, p. 32.)

6. Peters "The Day the Deities Return," p. 42.

7. In most traditions, the shaman calls in the directions moving sunwise, clockwise, further mimicking the motion of the cosmos.

8. Robert A. Johnson, *Inner Work: Using Dreams and Active Imagination for Personal Growth* (New York: HarperCollins, 1986), p. 102.

9. Secunda, May 3, 2000.

10. Ingerman, June 14, 2000.

11. *Encyclopedia Brittanica*, p. 783.

12. Eliade, *The Sacred and the Profane*, p. 88.

13. Ibid, p. 89.

14. Albert Villoldo, oral interview, April 20, 2000.

15. Adler, p. 154.

16. *Encyclopedia Brittanica*, p. 781.

17. Adler, p. 155.

18. Gershon Winkler, *Magic of the Ordinary: Recovering the Shamanic in Judaism* (Berkeley, Calif.: North Atlantic Books, 2003), p. 7.

19. Johnson, *Inner Work*, p. 100.

20. Ibid.

21. Ibid.

22. A Buddhist term for the spirits of dead ancestors who, for one reason or another, have not been guided to the afterlife and therefore roam the physical world homeless and hungry. In this case, the hungry ghosts were her old thought patterns, now exercised from her, who, once released, would want to reestablish themselves in the familiar comfort of her psyche.

Chapter 6

1. Ipupiara, oral interview, October 25, 2000.

2. Holgar Kalweit, *Shamans, Healers, and Medicine Men* (Boston: Shambala, 1987) p. 36.

3. Sandra Ingerman, *Soul Retrieval: Mending the Fragmented Self* (New York: HarperCollins, 1991), p. 14.

4. Vitebsky, *The Shaman*, p. 45.

5. Ingerman, *Soul Retrieval*, p. 200.

6. Roberta Louis, "Shamanic Healing Practices of the Ulchi," *Shaman's Drum* 53 (Fall 1999): 53.

7. Eliade, *Shamanism*, p. 300.

8. Secunda, June 14, 2000.

9. Ingerman, *Soul Retrieval*, p. 200.

10. Louis, "Shamanic Healing Practices," p. 55.

11. Ingerman, June 14, 2000.

12. Eliade, *Shamanism*, pp. 350–351.
13. Winkler, April 4, 2000.
14. Ibid.
15. Ipupiara, October 25, 2000.
16. Secunda, June 14, 2000.
17. Ipupiara, October 25, 2000.
18. Cowan, June 30, 2000.
19. Eliade, *Shamanism*, p. 442.
20. Miro-Quesada, July 25, 2000.
21. Carl Hyatt, oral interview, March 30, 2000.

Chapter 7

1. Joseph Campbell, *The Power of Myth*, p. 107.
2. Talbot, *The Holographic Universe*, p. 137.
3. Carl G. Jung, *Man and His Symbols* (New York: Anchor Press/Doubleday, 1964), p. 94.
4. Winkler, April 4, 2000.
5. Vitebsky, *The Shaman*, p. 18.
6. Although I have been using the term "seeing," this information may be perceived psychically in a variety of ways. Some perceive situations with claircognizance, an inner knowing, hunch, or intuition. Others, who are clairaudient, hear sounds, such as words or songs. Clairsentience causes some to perceive information through sensations in the physical body. Those with strengths in clairvoyance translate information visually and will often see pictures, either in the minds of high or even with eyes open. Likewise, others may receive information through taste and smell.
7. There is debate as to whether perception is entirely learned or whether perceptual learning is supplementary.
8. Frank J. Tipler, *The Physics of Immortality* (New York: Doubleday, 1994), p. 243.

9. Carlos Castaneda, *Tales of Power* (New York: Quality Paperback Bookclub, 1995), p. 530.

10. Brooke Medicine Eagle, oral interview, September 5, 2000.

11. Ken Eagle Feather, oral interview, July 12, 2000.

12. Richard D. Zakia, *Perceptual Quotes for Photographers* (Rochester, NY: Lighty Impressions Corporation, 1998) p. 93.

13. Mike Samuels, M.D. and Nancy Samuels, *Seeing with the Mind's Eye: The History, Techniques and Uses of Visualization* (New York: Random House, 1975), pp. 65–66.

14. Timothy Freke, *Shamanic Wisdomkeepers: Shamanism in the Modern World* (New York: Sterling Publishing Company, Inc., 1999), p. 14.

15. Ken Eagle Feather, July 25, 2000.

16. *The American Heritage Dictionary*, Fourth Edition (New York: Delta Trade Paperbacks, 2001), p. 442.

17. Bettina L. Knapp, *Anais Nin* (New York: Frederick Ungar Publishing Co., 1978), p. 1.

Afterword

1. Ipupiara, October 25, 2000.

2. Miro-Quesada, July 25, 2000.

3. "Grief and Praise: An Evening with Martin Prechtel" (audiotape). Sponsored by Hidden Wine Productions, February 20, 1997. Recorded in Minneapolis, Minn.

Resources

Teachers of Shamanism

Foundation for Shamanic Studies
P.O. Box 1939
Mill Valley, CA 94942
(415) 380–8282 (tel)
(415) 380–8416 (fax)
info@shamanism.org
www.shamanicstudies.org

A non-profit educational organization dedicated to the preservation, study, and transmission of shamanic knowledge. Led by Dr. Michael Harner, it is engaged in the revival and teaching of practical shamanism and shamanic healing. Its international faculty teaches training courses worldwide.

Dance of the Deer Foundation
Center for Shamanic Studies
P.O. Box 699
Soquel, CA 5073
(831) 475–9560 (tel)
(831) 475–1860 (fax)
info@shamanism.com
www.shamanism.com

Sponsors seminars, pilgrimages, and ongoing study groups throughout the world that are led by Brant Secunda, a recognized shaman in the tradition of the Huichol Indians of Mexico. They emphasize the importance of ceremony for personal well-being and for the continued survival of the environment and Mother Earth, and they provide a rare opportunity to experience Huichol Indian Shamanism. Participants in these programs take part in Huichol ceremonies, the sacred dance of the Deer, and pilgrimages to places of power and learn practices of shamanic health and healing.

The Sacred Trust
Wyld Hive House
St. Mary's Place
Penzance
Cornwall
TR18 4EE
(+44) 01736 331825 (tel)
mail@sacredtrust.co.uk
www.sacredtrust.org

A UK–based educational organization concerned with the teaching of practical shamanism for modern women and men. Founded by Simon Buxton, author of *The Way of the Bee*. Offers an ongoing curriculum of courses and training with The Foundation for Shamanic Studies. Offers a one-year training in Classical Shamanism, as well as some of the most challenging and profound ceremonial events, including sacred burial workshops, shamanic darkness workshops, and events with visiting teachers of note.

Larry G. Peters, Ph.D.
1212 Old Topanga Canyon Road
Topanga, CA 90290
(310) 455–2713 (tel)
lpshaman@aol.com

Offers workshops in the ancient shamanic tradition of Tibet, including pilgrimage and initiation journeys to Nepal.

Spirit Passages
www.spiritpassages.com

A joint practice of Evelyn C. Rysdyk, teacher of shamanism, artist, and author of *Modern Shamanic Living*, and C. Allie Knowlton, MSW, LCSW, DCSW, teacher of shamanism, and psychotherapist. Originally trained in core shamanism by noted anthropologist Michael Harner, Ph.D., and Sandra Ingerman, LMFT, LPCC, through the Foundation for Shamanic Studies Three Year Program, Allie and Evie have continued to expand their knowledge by working with indigenous teachers from Siberia, South America, and North America. Since 1991, they have offered shamanic workshops across the United States and Canada. In addition, they have worked with hundreds of people in their private shamanic healing practice, through referrals from doctors, psychotherapists, and other healthcare professionals.

Walking Stick Foundation
P.O. Box 1865
Cuba, New Mexico 87013
(505) 289–3344 (tel)
www.walkingstick.org

Dedicated to the recovery and preservation of indigenous spirituality. Offers programs in the aboriginal wisdom of Judaism, Native American, and other earth-honoring traditions.

Dr. Geo Cameron Trevarthen
Suite 120
12 South Bridge
Edinburgh
EH1 1DD
Scotland
tuath@celticshamanism.com
www.celticshamanism.com

Internet-, UK-, and Irish-based training in Celtic Shamanism, European Magickal Traditions, and Druidry from hereditary Celtic shaman priestess/holder of doctorate in anthropology and Celtic Studies from the University of Edinborough.

John Perkins
Dream Change Coalition
(561) 626–5662 (tel)
dreamchang@aol.com
www.dreamchange.org

Teaches workshops and apprenticeships on shamanism and rising to new levels of consciousness. Author of *Shapeshifting, The World is as You Dream It, Psychonavigation, The Stress-Free Habit,* and *Spirit of the Shuar.* Founder of Dream Change Coalition and seed-planter/board member of The Pachamama Alliance.

Aloha International
P.O. Box 223009
Princeville, HI 96722
(888) 827–8383 (tel)
www.huna.org

Teaches courses on Huna, Hawaiian shamanic healing, and lomi lomi nui. Offers free community events.

Alex Stark

270 5th Street, Room 1D

Brooklyn, NY 11215

(718) 840–2820 (tel)

(718) 832–1787 (fax)

alex@alexstark.com

www.alexstark.com

Consultation services in feng shui, geomancy, and shamanism. Offers workshops on The Path of Love and Power, an apprenticeship in practical spirituality utilizing knowledge, techniques, and processes borrowed from many different traditions, including native shamanism, Taoism, oriental feng shui, European geomancy, and the growing ecology movement.

Brooke Medicine Eagle

PMB C401

One Second Ave. E.

Polson, MT 59860

(406) 883–4686 (tel)

brooke@MedicineEagle.com

www.MedicineEagle.com

American native Earthkeeper, teacher, ceremonial leader, and author of *Buffalo Woman Comes Singing* and *The Last Ghost Dance*. Offers an in-depth training program, *Wakantia*, dedicated to teaching students to become Earth Mages living in harmony and with grace upon the Earth. Teaches and participates in international conferences and workshops, residential camps, and vision seeking.

Periodicals

Shaman's Drum
P.O. Box 270
Williams, OR 97544
(541) 846–1313 (tel)
sdrm@budget.net

A journal of experiential shamanism and spiritual healing published quarterly by the Cross Cultural Shamanism Network.

Index

About the Author

Hillary S. Webb has been studying the philosophies and practices of earth-based religions since the age of 10. As a way of deepening her understanding of the beliefs and techniques specific to shamanism, Webb spent several years interviewing more than two dozen shamans from both modern and indigenous cultures around the world. A compilation of these conversations will be published in the summer of 2004 entitled *Traveling Between the Worlds: Conversations on Contemporary Shamanism*. She lives in southern Maine.